THE SIERRA HIGH ROUTE

Traversing Timberline Country

THE SIERRA HIGH ROUTE

Traversing Timberline Country

STEVE ROPER

THE
MOUNTAINEERS

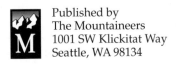
Published by
The Mountaineers
1001 SW Klickitat Way
Seattle, WA 98134

First printing 1997, second printing 2000, third printing 2004, fourth printing 2007, fifth printing 2009

Manufactured in the United States of America

Edited by Deborah Kaufmann
Maps (except topographic maps, pp. 207–230) by Nick Gregoric
All photographs by Steve Roper
Cover and book design by Alice C. Merrill

Cover photograph: North from Windy Ridge (Steve Roper)
Frontispiece: Lake near the South Fork of Cartridge Creek (Steve Roper)

Library of Congress Cataloging-in-Publication Data
Roper, Steve.
     The Sierra High Route : traversing timberline country / Steve Roper.
        p.   cm.
     Rev. ed. of: Timberline country. c1982.
     Includes bibliographical references (p.) and index.
     ISBN 0-89886-506-9
     1. Backpacking—Sierra Nevada (Calif. and Nev.)—Guidebooks.
2. Hiking—Sierra Nevada (Calif. and Nev.)—Guidebooks. 3. Sierra
Nevada (Calif. and Nev.)—Guidebooks. I. Roper, Steve. Timberline
country. II. Title.
GV199.42.S55R65 1997
917.94'40433—dc21   96-49269
                                                                             CIP

♻ Printed on recycled paper
ISBN: 978-0-89886-506-6

CONTENTS

Much of the charm of the mountains depends upon the absolute harmony of all that is there. There is no intrusive foreign thing in them; there is no inappropriate thing; there is no vulgar thing. They do not insolently thrust in your face silly placards . . . ; they do not disfigure themselves with lying real-estate signs; the names of no political candidates insult the trees; there are no yelping curs, blatant voices, or jangling street-cars; there is no odor of underground horrors or discomfort of dirty crowds. In the mountains all is large, quiet, pure, strong, dignified; there all is beautiful; each thing is a perfectly appropriate part of that unity which we call nature. . . . All is wholesome to the body, interesting to the mind, and agreeable to the senses. And the state of mind they tend to put us in may be called poetic.

— Bolton Coit Brown, from the January 1897 issue of the *Sierra Club Bulletin*

PREFACE

This guidebook is a revision of *Timberline Country: The Sierra High Route,* a book I wrote in 1982. After the book went out of print some years ago, backcountry enthusiasts began badgering me for copies and/or information. Only then did I realize how many people longed to do at least part of the route I had described that ran along the spine of California's Sierra Nevada. This new edition will, I hope, be welcomed by Sierra adventurers new and old.

I have made minor changes throughout and added material about current regulations, the too-detailed 7.5-minute maps, and two "new" problems: giardia and bears. As I age, the route seems, for some strange reason, more strenuous, and I have added warnings and advice that will be welcomed by graybeards and ignored by the pierced-ear crowd. As in the earlier book, I strongly recommend that beginners, traveling on their own, avoid this rugged route. Go with an experienced person—and be wary, anyway. Don't take this route lightly!

During the course of several summers in the late 1970s, I hiked every segment of the Sierra High Route at least once, gathering the descriptive material that forms the bulk of this guidebook. On most of these forays into the heart of the range I was accompanied by friends who, without overt complaining, tolerated my random wanderings through the subalpine landscape. Each of the following companions became intimately familiar with one or more sections of the route: Gilles Corcos, Marjorie Gelus, Dick Long, Larry Marino, Allen Steck, and Jim Wilson. To these friends—and especially to my wife, Kathy, who accompanied me on two-thirds of the route—I wish to express my appreciation. Their suggestions often led to an improvement in the course of the High Route, and their enchantment with the scenery confirmed my own feelings.

Though I spent several weeks in 1996 checking portions of the route, I have not recently covered its entire length. Here and there a

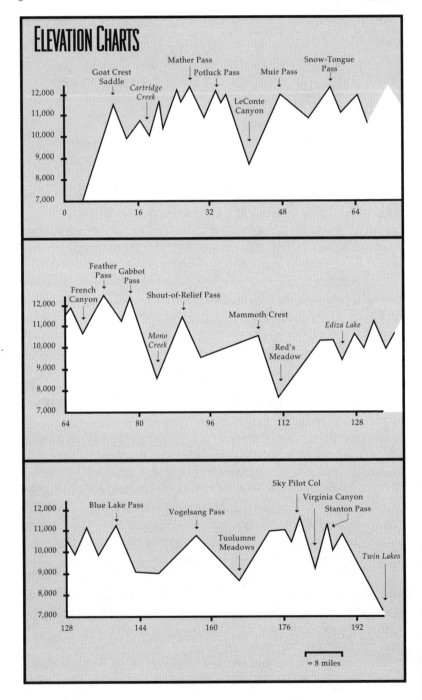

Elevation Charts

Goat Crest Saddle · *Cartridge Creek* · **Mather Pass** · **Potluck Pass** · **LeConte Canyon** · **Muir Pass** · **Snow-Tongue Pass**

12,000 · 11,000 · 10,000 · 9,000 · 8,000 · 7,000

0 · 16 · 32 · 48 · 64

French Canyon · **Feather Pass** · **Gabbot Pass** · **Shout-of-Relief Pass** · *Mono Creek* · **Mammoth Crest** · **Red's Meadow** · *Ediza Lake*

12,000 · 11,000 · 10,000 · 9,000 · 8,000 · 7,000

64 · 80 · 96 · 112 · 128

Blue Lake Pass · **Vogelsang Pass** · **Tuolumne Meadows** · **Sky Pilot Col** · **Virginia Canyon** · **Stanton Pass** · *Twin Lakes*

12,000 · 11,000 · 10,000 · 9,000 · 8,000 · 7,000

128 · 144 · 160 · 176 · 192

= 8 miles

rockfall or an avalanche may have squashed a few places. A few trail signs may have been added or removed. But trail signs are rare on this particular route, and the years fly by with little change to the topography. Hikers who use this book in conjunction with good maps and common sense will have a great time. During my recent research trips I was pleased, but not surprised, to see few traces of the passage of backpackers. Let's keep it that way.

Two stalwart backpackers recently plied me with information. Al Macdonald, my rock-climbing buddy from eons ago, has hiked much of the route, and his memory for detail is unsurpassed. He pointed out unclear passages in the original edition and suggested improvements. Because most of his trips involved extensive snowfields and/or bad weather, Macdonald alerted me to the special circumstances such travel requires (I usually enjoy perfect conditions, for some reason). Bill Schaefer, a Cal Tech research chemist, sent me much material about his adventures along the High Route, including a highly detailed fifty-seven-page pamphlet he had put together for his family and friends. Phrases such as "Roper wasn't too clear here" humbled me and made me dart for my old notes and visit tricky spots when I could. The book is far more accurate because of this new information. My thanks to both of these hardy mountain men.

To my 1996 companions Allen Steck and Kathy Roper once again, and my Sierra-wise cousin Louise Dunlap: thanks for your suggestions. As always, it's great fun to travel with appreciative companions.

Rangers who wander through the backcountry far more often than I do reviewed relevant parts of my manuscript and offered valuable advice about wilderness behavior, current regulations, and travel among the heights. These underpaid public servants work long hours, deal with emergencies that should never happen, pore over paperwork (such as my manuscript!), and spend far too little time in the place they love: the high mountains. My thanks to wilderness rangers John Ellsworth and Priscila Franco of Inyo National Forest; backcountry ranger George Durkee of Kings Canyon National Park; and backcountry ranger Mark Fincher of Yosemite National Park. From these four authorities I learned much about bear canisters, pH factors in streams, giardia cysts, fragile alpine soil, and other arcana. Though I incorporated virtually all of these experts' suggestions, I alone, of course, am responsible for the end result and any iconoclastic advice.

Quoted material is used throughout the book, especially in the historical overview. An enormous number of these quotations come from the *Sierra Club Bulletin*, usually the annual issue following the trip described. Rather than clutter the text with references to my sources, I have most often simply given the name of the book, magazine, or journal from which they came. A bibliography gives more detailed information.

In the interest of readability I have chosen to simplify certain technical details. For instance, I routinely imply that the High Route—and therefore the Sierra Nevada—runs in a north-south direction. The range, like the Pacific shoreline, actually tilts about thirty degrees off that convenient axis, trending in a direction that more closely approximates north-northwest by south-southeast. So, when I casually say to "move north," this generally means go uprange. When I specifically say to go "due north," this means straight up on the map; that is, true north, not magnetic north. Magnetic north is never used in this book.

I am aware, also, that the typical Sierra rock is not really granite; geologists use such words as granodiorite and quartz monzonite to describe the range's common rock. But, as naturalist Stephen Whitney has written, "The word *granite* has a long history of popular use predating the more restricted definition assigned to it by geologists."

In such place names as Red's Meadow and Devil's Postpile, I have used apostrophes even though they are missing in many guidebooks and all the official government maps. Cartographers dislike apostrophes for esoteric reasons, but I have heeded David Brower's forty-five-year-old advice: "Until someone can marshall sensible reasons against our doing so, we'll use the apostrophe just the way it should be used to make sense."

Finally, when exact elevations are not indicated on the topo maps, I have approximated them. A High Route pass, for example, might lie above the 11,280-foot contour line but below the next line, the one representing 11,360 feet. Technically, this pass should be shown as lying at 11,280+ feet, but I prefer to use the less awkward figure of, in this case, 11,300 feet.

Introduction

The timberline country of California's Sierra Nevada is dominated in summertime by five elements: meadowlands, gnarled trees, water, stone, and a cobalt sky occasionally augmented by towering cumulus clouds. In this austere landscape, backpackers who travel along the Sierra High Route—a rugged alternative to the John Muir Trail—can forget the outside world and concentrate solely on moving cross-country from one pristine campsite to another.

Although the popular John Muir Trail (shortened herein to Muir Trail) traverses this fascinating timberline country on occasion, it frequently descends west into heavily forested regions in order to circumvent the great ridges that jut out from the main Sierra crest. These diversions from what I regard as the range's finest terrain become especially annoying in the northern half of the High Sierra, for here the famed path traverses relatively lackluster country for many miles.

It occurred to me twenty years ago that if I scouted the range carefully I might be able to piece together a continuous route that would remain longer in timberline country than does the Muir Trail. Such a route, if feasible, would offer adventurous hikers an opportunity to visit superb country while simultaneously avoiding the multitudes of backpackers who prefer well-marked trails. In subsequent years I explored dozens of cirques and ridges, ending up in more cul-de-sacs than I care to remember. But eventually I evolved a marvelous 195-mile route that remains in close proximity to timberline, avoids major trails whenever possible, and yet requires no particular mountaineering skills. Almost all of what I call the Sierra High Route (most often shortened in this book to High Route) lies between 9,000 and 11,500 feet, that subalpine region fortuitously sandwiched between the dense western-slope forest and the ubiquitous granite blocks of the alpine zone.

Backpackers must not regard the High Route as an actual trail except for the sections in which it follows existing paths; the High Route traverses such rocky country that traces of human passage remain virtually undetectable. In this rugged landscape there's no "correct" route to hike, and each person naturally will choose a slightly different way. Similarly, in the far more fragile meadowlands through which the High Route occasionally passes, so many choices are available that paths are unlikely to be created except at those locations where the terrain forces hikers to funnel into one specific area. Even here, without the destructive hooves of pack animals to create deep trenches, the paths should remain inconspicuous. High Route adventurers will not be put off by the lack of an actual trail, since much of the singular joy of cross-country travel lies in wandering through the timberline country as the pioneers did—wondering what the next turn will reveal. Maintaining the pristine, trailless character of the High Route requires a conscious effort on the part of backpackers, and later in this introduction I discuss methods of preserving the fragile landscape.

The High Route begins in lovely Kings Canyon, that Yosemite-like gorge in the southern Sierra. I chose this location because it was the chief goal of the pioneers who, around the turn of the century, sought a high mountain route, passable to pack animals, from Yosemite southward (my first chapter relates some of the exploits of these pioneers). For two reasons, I believe the High Route is more practical when traveled from south to north, and it is so described. First, less snow falls in the southern half of the range than in the northern half; thus, intrepid hikers who plan to do the entire route will reach the zone of heavier snowpack later in the season, when the snow will have had additional time to melt. Second, by traveling northward, hikers generally walk away from the sun instead of into its blinding rays.

Climbing immediately from Kings Canyon some 6,000 feet to the Monarch Divide, the High Route then parallels this long ridge until it abuts the Sierra crest near Mather Pass. Three exceptionally lovely lake basins are encountered in the next thirty miles: Palisade, Dusy, and Evolution. After crossing the Glacier Divide, the High Route meanders across vast Humphreys Basin, then traverses the Bear Lakes region, the Mono Recesses, and the Silver Divide. Farther north, the route follows Mammoth Crest for a few miles before dropping abruptly to Devil's Postpile National Monument. The High Route then threads through the Ritter Range and enters Yosemite National Park

Major peaks, rivers, and approach roads of the High Sierra

via a remote pass near Foerster Peak. From this point the hiker follows seldom-traveled paths through Yosemite's backcountry to Tuolumne Meadows. The final segment of the High Route closely parallels the

Sierra crest, crossing it three times before reaching the route's northern terminus at Twin Lakes, near the village of Bridgeport.

Although the name *Sierra High Route* is mine, I make no claim for having pioneered a single step of the route. I first tramped through the Range of Light in 1954, a few decades too late to have explored virgin territory. Certain sections of what was to become the High Route have been described briefly in various guidebooks. On other segments I came across footprints and cairns, rather indisputable evidence that I was not first. Yet the conception of a continuous High Route—for humans, not pack animals—is probably mine, at least on paper.

Although I was personally delighted with my "discovery" of the High Route, I agonized for more than a year about whether or not to go public. The untrammeled nature of the timberline region had attracted me almost every summer for twenty-five years; why, I thought, should I advertise this paradise in a guidebook that would encourage numerous people to visit an area they otherwise might miss? Motives prove difficult to analyze, and, as Karl Marx once wrote, "The road to Hell is paved with good intentions." But in the end my incorrigible optimism prevailed; I was convinced that those backpackers capable of traversing the High Route's rugged and austere terrain would be the very ones who would leave no trace of their passage. From what I've seen recently, I think I was correct.

My chief concern while laying out the course of the High Route was to avoid excessively troublesome terrain. The difficulty of the 195-mile trek is necessarily subjective, for although mountaineers will find the route easy, neophytes could well have a rough time. Three categories adequately describe the type of travel encountered: trail walking, easy cross-country walking, and rugged cross-country travel.

Trail walking, often necessary on the High Route unless the hiker wishes to struggle over contrived routes, comprises nearly half the journey. The traveler follows the Muir Trail for a total of twenty-eight miles and more obscure paths for another sixty-five miles.

The major portion of the High Route—if one thinks in terms of time, not distance—traverses trailless but easy country. Meadowlands and granite slabs make up much of this distance, but solid, gently angled talus is also included (variously sized boulders, sharp-edged and stacked like dominoes, blanket the higher regions of the Sierra—this is talus). Few persons experienced in trail walking will have trouble with this type of terrain if they take their time.

A small percentage of the High Route's terrain falls into the category of onerous travel, usually involving steep and loose talus. These sections, most often encountered when crossing major east-west ridges, are not far in distance, but the hiker should expect to spend two or three hours on each crossing. No particular rock-climbing skills are required—and no ropes need be carried—but unsteady beginners with unwieldy packs will be ill at ease on such terrain. For this reason I strongly suggest that potential High Route travelers, if inexperienced on this type of terrain, spend some time in a less rugged part of the High Sierra prior to committing themselves to any lengthy portion of the trek. Later, I include hints on how to make cross-country walking of this type more pleasurable—or, phrased another way, less miserable.

Because of this occasionally rugged terrain, no group should ever set forth on the High Route without an experienced leader. Among other skills, this person must be well versed in interpreting topographic maps; be proficient at scrambling up and down class 3 rock (see the section called "Rating System" later in the Introduction for a definition); know first-aid procedures thoroughly; and be able to recognize the subtle signs that indicate a less experienced hiker is in trouble. By moving slowly, proffering tactful advice, and even lending a helping hand in a few rough spots, an experienced leader can safely shepherd a flock of novice mountaineers over any portion of the High Route.

Most backpackers will prefer to travel the High Route in sections rather than in its entirety, a month-long trek. Therefore, I have divided the route into five segments, each of which forms a chapter of the book. The end points of each segment either abut roads or are easily accessible from nearby ones. Each of the five segments will take most backpackers five or six days to hike, but it must be kept in mind that this estimate does not include the time spent approaching the High Route, enjoying rest days and side trips, or returning to the starting point. Thus, one easily might spend a ten-day vacation accomplishing each segment.

I have subdivided each route chapter into six sections. Each chapter opens with an overview highlighting the most interesting geographical and historical aspects of the route segment. An accompanying diagram enumerates the specific maps needed en route—these will be found at the back of the book.

Following this general description is an "Approaches" section, which describes how to reach either end of the segment. This section also outlines interesting loop trips that will enable the hiker to return to the starting point via a different route. These circuits should appeal to hikers who leave cars at a roadhead.

The bulk of each chapter describes the course of the High Route in general terms; detailed directions are rarely given in hopes that hikers will be adventurous enough to try the numerous possible variations. Similarly, campsites are never mentioned.

A brief section called "Reversing the Route" follows; it is designed to aid nonconformists planning to travel "backwards" along the High Route. Only places where the north-to-south traveler might encounter routefinding difficulties are described; details of the remainder of the route can be extrapolated from the main route description.

Next comes a section on "Alternate Routes." Since the hiker is hardly required to follow the High Route slavishly in order to travel through remarkable timberline country, these secondary routes, paralleling or diverting from the High Route, should be considered by all travelers. Some of these alternate routes involve crossing more difficult terrain than is found on the High Route itself while some entail less strenuous walking. All alternates prove interesting, and some reach extremely remote regions well worth visiting. Furthermore, using alternate routes will help reduce the impact on the landscape.

Finally, a section called "Mountaineering" describes enjoyable, nontechnical climbs that can be reached easily from the High Route. Venturesome hikers will enjoy remarkable panoramas from these summits.

CROSS-COUNTRY TRAVEL

As mentioned earlier, much of the High Route involves cross-country travel, a type of hiking significantly different from normal trail walking. Perhaps the greatest dissimilarity between the two types concerns the walker's rhythm. The consistent, relaxed strides favored by those who travel well-maintained trails are replaced, in rugged terrain, by irregular movements of the feet and continual body shifts that alter balance.

These important adjustments of rhythm and technique cannot be learned from a book; competence in any sport is attained only by practice. While the rudiments of such city sports as tennis or bowling can be learned relatively quickly because of readily available facilities and instructors, few persons have the time, opportunity, or patience to practice cross-country hiking. Rather, the tendency is for the neophyte to go out and *do* it, solving problems as they arise, without benefit of formal instruction. This casual approach seems admirable to me, for in the end it proves more rewarding to discover techniques on one's own than to be told at every juncture what one is doing wrong. Still, cross-country hiking of the variety encountered on the more rugged portions of the High Route can be made safer and more enjoyable if hikers absorb the basic lessons a book can furnish. The advice that follows is given with one overriding thought in mind: a trip without traumas is bound to be a pleasurable one.

Perhaps the prime piece of advice for beginners is to start hiking early each day and move slowly, but inexorably, toward the next campsite. Unpleasant experiences often result from being tired and pressed for time at the end of a strenuous day. Don't attempt long distances at first, especially if the terrain exceeds 11,000 feet, where the thin air adversely affects the stamina and judgment of unacclimated hikers. Those backpackers who are not compelled to race the sinking sun are more likely to enjoy their adventure.

However carefully one plans the itinerary, the day's journey will not be carefree if one is burdened with inferior or unnecessary equipment. Although the cross-country hiker's gear closely approximates that of the trail walker, the traveler should reevaluate his or her equipment with the more demanding terrain in mind. The two most important items to reexamine are boots and packs.

Lightweight shoes suitable for trail walking may not give the talus walker enough support; indeed, they may even fall apart before the journey is completed. Boots constructed with heavier materials and thicker soles will prove superior on much of the High Route's rugged terrain.

Regardless of the weight carried, frame packs constructed with aluminum tubing are usually top-heavy, and as the hiker lurches through talus, the rigid load can shift abruptly and throw him or her off balance. Doug Robinson, editor of the latest edition of *Starr's Guide to the John Muir Trail*, aptly calls these frame packs "equilibrium destroyers." Frameless packs—or packs with nonrigid internal frames—prove

superior for cross-country travel because they cannot shift independently of the body. The hiker in the market for a new pack should
consider the frameless styles. In addition to their nonshifting charac-
teristics, frameless packs admirably substitute as daypacks, a boon to
hikers who plan side trips while on a backpacking journey. Frameless
packs do have one drawback: they are not as comfortable as their rigid
counterparts. Resting directly against the body, they quickly trap the
sweat from one's back, thus causing a hot, sticky feeling.

Break camp at dawn, strap on sturdy boots and a comfortable
pack, and all will go well, right? Hardly, for the traveler soon faces
the first of the myriad daily decisions: which way to go? The general
directions given in this guide are intended solely to free the hiker from
having to make *major* decisions. Solving a specific routefinding problem is such an enjoyable and rewarding exercise that it would be inappropriate to describe the High Route step-by-step, even if this were
possible.

It follows, then, that at least one member of the party must be
willing and able to make routefinding decisions at every stage of the
journey. This person must plan ahead, not only for the next several
steps, but sometimes for a mile at a time. Which side of the lake has
less talus? Which of several notches on the ridge above appears easiest, and what might lie on the other side—a cliff or easy ledges? These
judgments are hardly of a cosmic nature; a "wrong" choice might result in a brief retreat or an unnecessary elevation change of fifty feet.
Nevertheless, leaders proud of their routefinding abilities will strive
to avoid even minor errors, with the subtle result that the party should
feel less tired and thus more animated at the end of each day.

Becoming competent at finding the most desirable route, the traveler soon learns, is chiefly a matter of practice. Still, some strategies
can be learned in advance. One easily learned tactic involves scan-
ning the upcoming terrain, especially from high places, and memo-
rizing specific landmarks. Such markers, of course, will change both
in shape and prominence as the hiker approaches them.

Understanding something of the Sierra's geography can also
enable the leader to choose the most appropriate route. For instance,
willows often choke valleys below 9,000 feet. Talus tends to be unstable above 11,500 feet. The High Route traverses the zone between
these two elevations as much as possible, but during approaches to,
and departures from, the route, such potentially unpleasant terrain

may be avoided if the problem is recognized in advance. The traveler should also be aware that north- and east-facing slopes are usually steeper than their opposite sides and can also harbor dangerous snow and ice. Thus, when traveling north on the High Route (with such slopes hidden from view), knowledge of this fact can help hikers traverse problematic places on their easier sides. For instance, bypass that small bluff ahead on the left, if feasible—that way should have less snow and be lower angled.

Even though much of the High Route passes through gentle terrain upon which the walking resembles that done on a trail, the traveler occasionally encounters rugged spots where the feet must be placed with precision, both for efficiency's sake and to avoid injury. This technique is especially necessary when clambering through steep talus. The traveler frequently comes across granite blocks so precariously perched that a phantom's breath could send them tumbling. While a nudge from a hiker's pack might be all it takes to send such a boulder into the void, more often it is the hiker's foot that is responsible. If a rock is dislodged, the perpetrator can suffer a frightening and painful fall, simultaneously cascading stones onto hikers below.

To avoid such a traumatic incident, simply bypass any loose-looking rocks. When ascending talus, this is rather easy to do, for by taking a few moments to test suspicious boulders, it is possible to choose the most secure blocks. A ski pole comes in handy here, for one can prod ahead when needed. But when heading downhill, it is difficult to determine if the next foothold is stable, since gravity and momentum—those inexorable demons—dictate that the hiker make abrupt movements over terrain that cannot be studied much in advance. It follows that the descent of a talus slope is much more demanding than its ascent—and a lot harder on the knees!

Even an experienced talus hopper occasionally sends a block on its way. This awesome event, however, rarely causes panic, for the instant the boulder begins to roll, the expert is gliding toward an optional foothold that was routinely catalogued in the brain milliseconds earlier. The cry "Rock!" is airborne even before the new landing spot is reached. This instinctively shouted alarm informs hikers below to dart instantly toward a sheltered niche catalogued in *their* brains milliseconds earlier. Or else those below are purposely spread out far enough from the fall line to enjoy the ensuing rumbling dispassionately.

Such confidence does not come easily. How does the hiker learn to move adroitly down what Doug Robinson has called a "sea of holes"? How does he or she develop the leg strength necessary to absorb the cartilage-rending shocks received when moving efficiently down the obstacle course? Practicing talus walking is about as agreeable as practicing bivouacking, but beginners will have a more rewarding High Route experience if they endure a day of training. For the first lesson, choose a low-angled talus slope. Without a pack, work slowly up and then down a hundred-yard course, then return and attempt the downward passage with more flair. Note that the feet stick to amazingly steep chunks of rock if they remain there for only a fraction of a second. Notice how one teeters when moving slowly; appreciate how this potentially unsafe condition vanishes as the speed of descent increases. Finally, undertake the course with a pack, noting the disheartening loss of maneuverability. Once this gentle slope has been mastered, move on to a steeper incline to refine the techniques.

In time the novice will come to recognize the varying quality of footholds. For instance, small stones precariously balanced near the outer edges of talus blocks must be avoided at all costs. Similarly, sand or gravel on a sloping hold present an insidious hazard. The hiker soon learns that the smooth, flat surfaces of large boulders provide the most obvious and secure foot placements. Other excellent holds can be found in the V-shaped slot where two or more boulders meet. Not only is the foot nicely supported in this gap, but if one boulder begins to shift, the hiker gains a precious extra moment to make the transition to another block. A downside of this technique is that one can get a foot stuck in the V!

During the course of a talus scramble, the hiker's hands and arms contribute much more than might be expected. On steep talus the heel of the hand often acts as a braking mechanism as the crouching hiker descends a sloping boulder. A stiffened arm can be used to bridge a gap, allowing the hiker to swing a leg to a lower hold. Cross-pressure techniques, where arms span gaps to maintain balance, come into play constantly.

Granite slabs are perhaps the single most aesthetic feature of timberline country, and they can be as easy to walk across as a sidewalk. But when they steepen, or display a scattering of sand, they can prove disconcertingly slippery. These slabs are rarely continuous, and the hiker who plans ahead can wander about by means of the narrow ledges that so often interrupt them. If a steep slab must be climbed, remember to keep the weight directly over the feet. When descending steep slabs, resist the temptation to sit down and slide; this inelegant tactic will shred one's clothing as well as one's dignity. If the slab appears to be so steep and exposed that upright walking would be foolhardy, simply squat and use flat-foot placements in conjunction with both palms. Moving one limb at a time, slowly shuffle downward. This stable posture should allow the hiker to descend all but the steepest slabs, the ones best left to confident rock climbers.

High Route travelers who trek earlier than about August 1 may encounter extensive snowfields, far more treacherous terrain than either talus or slabs. Numerous Sierra backpackers have been injured when they lost control on steep snowfields and careened into the talus below. If the snow is rock hard—as it is early in the morning or in shaded couloirs—*never* venture onto it without an ice ax and a rope. Luckily, many High Route snowfields can be bypassed after midseason; those that can't should be attempted *only in the afternoon,* when the snow is soft. Of course, not all snowfields are dangerous; low-angled ones with gradually tapering runouts allow far easier walking than the trekker would find in the nearby talus. And, once in a great while, the experienced hiker will be able to enjoy glissading, that thrilling activity akin to skiing without skis.

Snowfields don't need to be steep to be treacherous. Lurking beneath that seemingly solid surface are holes and caves. Hikers who break through into one of these will regret it: jagged rocks and frigid streams will cause serious problems. In snow-filled valleys keep away from low points, where a silent stream may well have undercut the snow, leaving only a thin bridge. Look ahead for streams entering or leaving snowfields and plan the route accordingly. Similarly, take care when nearing isolated rocks and trees sticking up out of the snow. Snowfield edges can be treacherous also—they are often undercut. A ski pole prodding ahead like Superman's X-ray vision is a valuable tool on such terrain.

Stream crossings conclude this brief accounting of potentially hazardous terrain. Along the High Route these generally prove insignificant, for the traveler fords most creeks near their sources, where they are only yards wide. But there are exceptions, especially in the early season when the creeks churn tumultuously toward the lowlands. If a fallen log or a stream-spanning series of boulders cannot be located, one must wade. Here is the place to don a pair of light-weight camp shoes, for the rocks can be both sharp and slippery. One person should scout a major crossing without a pack, first establishing that no rapids lurk immediately downstream. Unsteady hikers should have their packs transported across by the more confident ones. *Never* tie into a rope anchored upstream and try to "pendulum" across a fast-flowing river: the laws of physics dictate that a taut rope can easily force one to the bottom, there to remain helpless until death mercifully comes. A rope stretched straight across a stream and used only as a hand line, however, can be a godsend.

TREADING SOFTLY

As the High Route becomes increasingly popular, hikers must adopt certain tactics if the fragile landscape is to remain in the same condition as when the pioneers passed through it. Much of the potential damage to the timberline country—such as the creation of new trails, the pollution of water, and the degradation of campsites—can be prevented if travelers follow a few basic guidelines.

Faint paths are likely to evolve in such places as lakeshores, where each traveler tends to follow the same track. But in most of the High Route's meadowlands, the hiker can avoid creating even a semblance of a path by choosing a route that, by skirting the meadow, remains far from delicate streamside vegetation. By stepping on rock or gravel as much as possible and on wet areas as little as possible, one leaves barely a trace. When descending a scree slope beneath a pass, the hiker should zigzag down the sides of the fall line to avoid creating an unsightly trench that thunderstorm runoff or snowmelt will further erode.

Piles of rocks, called *ducks* or *stone men,* also contribute to the establishment of new trails. Over a period of half a century, well-intentioned hikers have built thousands of these markers to help subsequent travelers find their way over rough sections of the High Sierra. The elaborately constructed monuments tend to channel hikers onto the exact same route, where a path soon develops. In all likelihood the ducked path is neither easier nor more direct than numerous alternate routes a few score feet distant. Ducks also detract from the wilderness experience and can lull one into complacency. For all these reasons I recommend that High Route backpackers dismantle ducks wherever they are found—unless there's a *very* good reason for them.

Each backpacker must observe proper methods of wilderness sanitation. Two rules must always be followed when defecating: choose a site several hundred feet—or farther—from the nearest water, and deposit the waste in a hole that can be covered completely with soil or rocks. This is difficult to do in the rocky timberline region, but try. And try also to avoid damaging alpine plants during the excavations. Such measures help preserve the fragile environment and ensure that feces will not be washed down into the water supply by rainwater or dug up by animals.

Used toilet paper should be packed out when possible—this is a requirement in Yosemite National Park. One can also burn toilet paper if, and only if, the conditions are safe, as in a talus field or in an existing fire ring. Never burn the paper in a forest: serious fires have resulted.

One should also avoid contaminating streams with soap and food, as this doesn't sit well with the creatures that depend on the water

A frantic stream

supply. Perform all dishwashing chores and personal ablutions far from the banks of a stream or lake. Even biodegradable soap should not get into the water supply; it can cause eutrophication equally well as regular soap.

Most of the visible damage to the environment takes place in the vicinity of campsites. Popular places in the High Sierra show grievous scars from generations of campers. Bare-dirt patches indicate where hikers have set up tents; flame-blackened boulders testify to once-roaring campfires; trash and human waste encroach upon campsites; and ancient pine snags, once beautiful, have been rendered desolate by seekers of wood. In popular locales where many such sites are clustered together, the drinking water is suspect, pack animals have churned the nearby meadows into fetid bogs, and hikers camp within yards of one another. The mere existence of these "slums"—occupied or not—means that an important aspect of the wilderness experience has vanished.

Fortunately, the above-described damage remains absent from most High Route campsites, and it must stay this way forever. For this reason, individual campsites are never mentioned in this guide, which is a departure from most guidebooks dealing with a specific mountain area. Instead of reading about campsites, travelers will have to choose them in a more imaginative fashion. This will not prove much of a hardship, however, for the High Route hiker is assured of discovering a comfortable spot almost anywhere in flat areas near water below the 10,800-foot level in the southern half of the range, and below the 10,200-foot mark in the northern half. Numerous possibilities are apparent to anyone who studies the topo map in advance; when arriving at a possible area, it does not take long to find an ideal site. Hikers who choose locations never before used for camping will not only feel like pioneers, they also will have the satisfaction of leaving the site unsullied, an impossibility in an already damaged location.

To preserve the quality of these remote, pristine campsites—and to avoid further harm to already damaged ones—hikers should practice common sense while traveling the High Route. A few suggestions are given below; rangers can also provide useful information.

Campsites should always be established as far as practical from any sources of drinking water; this preserves the quality of the water as well as saving the fragile streamside meadows from the inevitable trampling campsites receive. (The present law: camp at least 100 feet from water, but the farther the better.) Avoid camping on fragile vegetation; instead choose a bare-dirt patch or a gravelly area. Those who carry several water containers can camp in beautiful spots far from water, thus avoiding people and mosquitoes while helping preserve the most fragile part of the High Sierra.

Although the pioneers "rearranged" their camps to suit their needs, the present-day hiker should read about such practices, not emulate them. The day has long passed when the traveler can, with impunity, construct windbreaks and tent platforms, or cut pine boughs for a bed.

Firewood has become so scarce in timberline country—and the remaining pine snags are so picturesque—that the camper should *never* build a campfire above the 9,000-foot level. If, for atavistic reasons, one must have a fire at lower altitudes, then use an existing fire ring, gather only downed wood, and keep the fire small. The modern gas stove is a marvelous, lightweight piece of equipment, and its use everywhere should be regarded as a badge of honor among High Route trekkers.

Needless to say, all garbage must be packed out of the high country; only a lazy or uninformed person buries or tries to burn cans, aluminum foil, orange peels, and the like. An exception: small remnants of food left in bowls and pots should be buried or thrown on the ground away from the stream. There is nothing less aesthetic than the sight of noodles reposing on a stream bottom like albino eels. Furthermore, these nutrients upset the balance of life in the water—a balance that took eons to develop.

Finally, a word about group size. In the old days huge groups (more than 150 people sometimes!) visited the high country and stayed for weeks. The damage that resulted could be seen decades later. Large groups are now highly discouraged, and some areas have a maximum of eight. A party of two to four seems perfect to me; the campsite won't be crowded; the noise level will be low; and the land will not be trampled unduly.

All of the above-mentioned guidelines lead to one axiom: leave no trace. Simply walk gently through the wilderness by day and sleep lightly upon it by night. And, while doing so, imagine the thrill of returning some day to discover that no visible change has taken place.

THE WATER

In a region once famed for the purity of its water, the recent discovery of pollution in High Sierra streams is particularly shocking. Every hiker suffers either directly or indirectly from this contamination, lending validity to the cliché about the absurdity of soiling one's own nest. Researchers have discovered coliform bacteria—a sure indication of human feces—in many Sierra streams. Diseased animals also defecate in the watershed. Nasty parasites and bacteria may be floating about, and it's impossible for a hiker to predict their presence or absence.

An optimist drinks Sierra water straight, without thought. A pessimist imagines that the same stream is teeming with death-dealing critters. It's clear that one *can* get sick from various bugs, but no meaningful statistics tell us what percentage of Sierra travelers who drink the water straight suffer afterward.

Although more serious diseases than giardiasis are possible, it is this disease that worries most hikers. In a 1984 study, scientists found giardia cysts in one-third of sixty-nine tested Sierra lakes and streams. Apparently one must ingest a minimum of ten cysts even to have a chance of getting sick, and the study found that the highest concentration discovered was forty-one cysts per hundred gallons of water. The next highest was fourteen. Both these sites were heavily used ones, and, for the High Route traveler, the good news is that streams in high, remote basins have far fewer cysts than do lower streams. Thus, the chance of contracting the disease up high seems virtually nil. On an anecdotal basis, this is further demonstrated: I have never had the disease, though for forty years I've most often drunk the water straight. George Durkee, a backcountry ranger in Kings Canyon National Park for more than twenty years, has never heard of a giardia case. Longtime Sierra mountaineer and giardia expert Bob Rockwell wrote me: "Most of the water in the Sierra has far too few giardia cysts for you to contract an infestation. Even if the water has many cysts you probably won't get the disease. If you do, you probably won't have any symptoms. If you get symptoms they will probably go away by themselves in a week or so. If they don't, or you develop serious persistent symptoms, you should seek medical treatment."

Good sanitation may also prevent giardiasis: it is certain that asymptomatic carriers spread the disease unknowingly (cooks and food handlers are most often the guilty ones). And one out of five people are giardia carriers, it is surmised. A recent article in the *Journal of Wilderness and Environmental Medicine* claims that a majority of giardiasis is caused by fecal-oral or foodborne transmission. Thus, those who get giardiasis shouldn't necessarily blame the water.

As it is entirely possible that giardia cysts are more common now than they were a few years ago, it is best to play it safe and sterilize all drinking water, especially in popular places or where pack animals have trod. Rangers recommend three methods, all foolproof for giardiasis: filtering, iodine treatment, or boiling. Using this latter method, keep the water boiling for several minutes; 190 degrees kills giardia cysts instantly but nastier bugs survive a little longer (at 10,500 feet, water boils at 193 degrees).

SEASONS

Three phrases are used in this book to define the average seasonal conditions to be expected by High Route travelers. These phrases—early season, midseason, and late season—are arbitrary, depending as they do upon the previous winter's snowfall, the intensity of the spring's sunshine, and the pattern of autumn storms. For example, during the unusual drought of 1977–79, hikers wandered throughout the High Sierra, easily avoiding snowfields, as early as mid-June. But during the summer of 1983, and again in 1995, the snowpack was immense and slow to melt, with the result that even in late August hikers had to descend dangerous snowfields and cross raging creeks.

Early season, as defined in this guide, includes both June and July, a time when snow usually forms a dominant part of the Sierra scene. This snow can be rock hard in morning, and thus dangerous; it can be knee-deep by late afternoon, and thus contribute to fatigue. Suncups can be of nightmarish size and sharpness. Snowy slopes and gullies on the north and east flanks of ridges can cause untold problems and dangers for hikers unaccustomed to such terrain. An ice ax can prove useful—but learn how to use it first. A ski pole, useful for balance on snow, is mandatory for neophytes. The weather can be unstable in June, and minor storms often deposit several inches of snow atop the melting snowpack. Crossing swollen streams proves tricky and even dangerous. Fragile meadows, when not covered with snow, can be easily damaged quagmires. One often moves at half-speed in early season. However, there *are* advantages to traveling at this time of year: few hikers are encountered, mosquitoes are not yet aggressive, and gently sloped snowfields offer far easier traveling than the slabs or talus beneath. All in all, however, hikers without a highly experienced leader should plan on avoiding the High Route during June and July because of the insidious problems associated with snow. The potential dangers cannot be emphasized strongly enough; call a ranger station in late April to learn if the snowpack is slight, average, or huge—and plan the trip accordingly.

Midseason, here defined as the period from August 1 to Labor Day, traditionally has been the most popular time of year to visit the high country. The snow cover has disappeared, except on the north sides of passes. Wildflowers have burst forth in profusion, some-times covering acres of meadowland. The weather remains so stable that the adage "It never rains at night in August in the Si-erra" has some validity. Occasional afternoon thun-derstorms contribute to the beauty of the range while si-multaneously dissipating the haze. Mosquitoes have become a nuisance, but at least they have numerous victims from whom to choose, for the mountains are teeming with backpack-ers, especially on the estab-lished trails.

Shooting stars (Dodecatheon jeffreyi)

Late season, covering the interval from Labor Day to the first significant autumn snowfall, can be an excellent time to wander along the High Route. The crowds have returned to the cities, and the frigid night air has rendered the remain-ing mosquitoes apathetic.

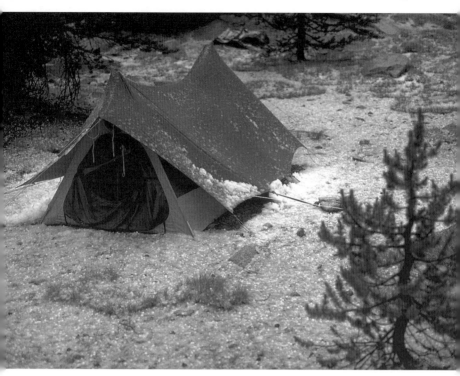

Aftermath of a thirty-minute hailstorm

The summer haze has vanished, and from certain High Route passes it is possible to identify peaks ninety miles distant. The chief disadvantage of late-season travel concerns the uncertainty of the weather. A major storm often strikes the Sierra Nevada during the first part of September. This tempest, sometimes displaying a brutal intensity (in 1978 such a storm killed three Sierra backpackers), can deposit a foot of snow above the 10,000-foot level and ushers in the less predictable autumn climate. As this storm fades, the weather settles into an uneasy Indian summer, during which cold, clear spells can be interrupted by relatively benign intervals of rain and light snowfall. Since this snow melts quickly upon resumption of fine weather, it causes little trouble for the High Route traveler prepared to pause for a day or two. Nevertheless, those who plan to venture into the high country after Labor Day should carry warm clothing, a storm-proof tent, and extra food.

Late season gradually evolves into winter; by early November freshly fallen snow no longer melts, and the wind howls. Only competent mountaineers familiar with alpine hazards have any business traveling the High Route from November to mid-May. By mid-April, when most of the avalanche danger has passed, the less rugged portions of the High Route will appeal to experienced cross-country skiers.

BEARS

Bears belong in the mountains; we are the intruders. Large wild animals are becoming rare in North America, and we want and need them in our wilderness. It is fairly easy to coexist with black bears in the Sierra, yet we must keep them from our food if they are to remain wild and skeptical of humans. Bears that habitually garner food from unknowledgeable tourists and backpackers become aggressive and are executed. This is not right.

Grizzlies have been extinct in California for seventy-five years, and the following advice deals only with the much smaller and generally less aggressive black bear. These foothill beasts were once extremely rare in timberline country, but recently they have been seen as high as 11,500 feet, even on the dry east side of the range. Luckily, this species is not dangerous to humans unless a female with cubs is surprised. To avoid such a confrontation, one should make extra noise when thrashing through willow thickets and dense forests.

People food is the main problem with bears. They love it. Fortunately, several methods exist to keep food and bear from meeting. Yet bears seem to be getting smarter as the years go by, and one often hears campfire stories that make the ursines out to be as clever as apes. Take heed: this is almost true.

One method of storage that works perfectly is to place food in the large, hard plastic containers that can be rented from certain ranger stations and outdoors outlets. These are bulky and heavy—the last thing one wants to carry on a long backpack. But since no bear will ever get into one, definitely consider this device for short trips. Shortly, this canister could be mandatory equipment in the three national parks of the High Sierra. Government intrusion, yes, but certainly in the bears' best interest. Perhaps someone will soon develop a truly lightweight container; this would then become the standard foolproof method of foiling the animal.

Until this happens, long-term hikers who camp in heavily wooded areas should hang their food in the manner now suggested by rangers. Two counterbalanced food sacks are arranged to dangle from a high tree limb, far out from the trunk, with no cords dropping downward (rangers have handouts showing this method). Even when set up perfectly, this method often fails unless used in conjunction with yelling and screaming, so make sure tent and tree are fairly near each other. A rattled bear won't have the patience for figuring out a new way to circumvent the hiker's cleverness. In the same vein, hurling baseball-sized stones into the rump of the beast will not hurt it—but should cause it to flee and try its luck elsewhere. Obviously, never get so aggressive toward a sow with cubs.

Higher, at timberline, this hanging trick is impossible because of the stunted trees, so at night one should store the food about thirty feet from camp, rigged with "burglar alarms" of balanced cooking pots. Upon hearing a commotion, begin yelling and immediately dash toward the scene with as much noise as possible. Use a flashlight to scan for cubs.

Other methods of hiding food have been tried, but Yosemite backcountry ranger Mark Fincher has a warning: "All other food storage methods I've heard suggested—burying food in rocks, hanging it off boulders, stashing it on islands, and countless other creative 'solutions'—simply do not work. The bear usually gets the food in a matter of seconds, not nearly enough time for a camper to wake up, put on shoes, and chase the bear away."

Bears are mostly nocturnal, but on day trips away from a timberline camp one can't just leave the food in the tent or backpack. As a "whistling in the dark" solution, maybe it's best to find a small hole in the talus, stash the food, and seal the entrance with huge rocks placed in such as way as to have a keystone that requires more than ten IQ points to remove. This trick will at least make one feel better—and it will also discourage marmots and ground squirrels.

Many campers, especially in the lowlands, have awoken to find a bear's fetid breath mingling with their own. To avoid this unsettling experience, sleep at some distance from the cooking area, keep the sleeping bag and tent absolutely free from food odors, and don't wear food-stained clothing to bed. Don't use perfumes and deodorants, either, for bears seek these out as if they were honey.

One last bit of advice: when confronting a black bear without cubs, be aggressive. If a battle ensues, never play dead; this technique works (sometimes) only with grizzlies.

SAFETY

Unlike most of the other mountainous regions of North America, the High Sierra in summer is a gentle wilderness indeed. Absent are the shattered glaciers, killer storms, friable rock, and unpredictable grizzlies that make hiking and mountaineering in the Canadian Rockies, for instance, a far more dangerous proposition. Nevertheless, serious hazards exist in the Sierra, and the High Route traveler should be forewarned.

Responsible leaders of High Route trips should make sure that everyone understands the consequences of an accident in the remote high country. A relatively minor accident, such as a broken ankle, will prove traumatic to the victim and ruin the trip for the others. Furthermore, as mountaineering accidents increase and rangers and sheriffs become overburdened, authorities are now fining backpackers who must be rescued because of abject stupidity (for example, getting hypothermia by wearing cotton clothes and not having a tent in a bad storm in October). The Code of Federal Regulations provides for such behavior: the infraction is called Disorderly Conduct/Creating a Hazardous Condition, and numerous rock climbers in Yosemite Valley have been fined ($13,325 was the highest levy in 1996—a big storm on El Capitan, no rain gear, and forty rescuers involved). Hikers should assume personal responsibility for their actions and consider self-rescue unless an accident is life threatening. One must also keep in mind that rescuers die each year in this country because of foolish mistakes made by those who do not respect the potential dangers of the outdoors.

Group members who wish to enjoy a safe trip should stick closely to their leader, never straying onto more difficult terrain. A hiker who feels threatened by the terrain at any point should speak out *immediately;* no one who realizes the consequences of an accident will think this a cowardly act.

Those unfortunates who get separated and lost should stay put. Easier said than done, but all a search party has to go on is one simple fact: where was the person last seen? One who wanders far from that spot could end up a skeleton.

Specific safety problems connected with loose talus, slippery slabs, steep snowfields, and stream crossings have been dealt with in the earlier section entitled "Cross-country Travel." An additional hazard concerns mountaineering along the High Route. While the route itself involves no technical climbing—that is, ropes are not necessary—the most appealing nearby peaks require certain rock-climbing skills. Hikers untrained in these skills often set out frivolously to reach such summits, and tragedy can result. Dangers lurk everywhere on steep rock: handholds can break, the climber can slip off a scree-covered ledge, or fall while negotiating an icy patch in a shaded gully. If the exposure is great enough, the fall can prove fatal. Attempting to ascend steep terrain without having gained experience on class 4 rock can only be called foolhardy.

Traveling solo along the High Route can be an enjoyable, almost mystical, experience. But all solo wanderers should leave their exact itineraries with a responsible friend, for even a sprained ankle can have major consequences, especially in the off-season, when only five people a week may be encountered along the route.

Hikers who travel in early or late season should be aware of that insidious killer known as hypothermia. The typical scenario for death by exposure begins when an exhausted hiker pushes his or her limits during cold or windy weather. The first symptoms include an inability to keep warm, unusual weakness, and excessive grouchiness soon followed by fits of uncontrollable shivering. When this shivering tapers off and finally ceases, death is imminent. All this can happen in the space of a few hours.

It is obvious that one must recognize this life-threatening condition early in its subtle progress. Since the person who has hypothermia is usually the last to realize it, a competent leader should monitor all members of the party during cold or windy weather, watching especially for laggards who exhibit unusual behavior. A person who becomes thoroughly chilled, inexplicably tired, and uncharacteristically irritable probably has hypothermia. The party should stop immediately and set up a tent or windproof shelter. The victim should remove all clothes, dart into a sleeping bag, and be given hot drinks and high-energy food. If the hypothermia has progressed to the uncontrollable-shivering stage, another hiker should strip and get into the same sleeping bag; the transfer of heat can effect a dramatic improvement in the condition of the victim.

If hypothermia is treated during its early stages, the victim will be quite ready to travel the following day. In more serious cases, escort the person from the high country as soon as possible.

Acute mountain sickness (AMS) can pose a problem to those High

Route travelers who move quickly from sea level to 10,000 feet and above. Because less oxygen is available at high altitudes, the balance between water and electrolytes in the body is affected in ways not fully understood. Symptoms of the illness include headache, loss of appetite, nausea, and uneasy sleep. According to Dr. Charles Houston, an expert in the field of mountain sickness, the overall feeling is "very much like a bad hangover." Most persons will be fully protected from AMS if they take a full day to reach each successive 1,000 feet above the 7,000-foot level. Using this formula, one can see that at 13,000 feet the average person requires about one week to reach the point where strenuous exertion produces no ill effects. At this altitude, however, it takes at least one year before one acclimates fully and thus regains sea-level performance.

If the High Route traveler experiences AMS, there is only one practical solution, the same one recommended for hangovers: wait it out. Banish thoughts of climbing higher (descending will help) and drink copious quantities of liquid. A day of complete inactivity should alleviate most symptoms, although they could recur if the victim attempts to climb higher too quickly.

If time cures AMS, the opposite is true for another, far more consequential, form of altitude sickness. Death can come quickly to those unfortunates who suffer from high-altitude pulmonary edema (HAPE) and remain at high altitude. Although rare below 9,000 feet, the disease has struck numerous Sierra travelers at elevations not much higher. Early symptoms of HAPE include severe shortness of breath, inexplicable weakness, mental confusion, and a pulse rate of 100 or more. Vomiting may occur and headaches may be violent or absent. When the disease is well along, a gurgling or bubbling sound emanating from the lungs is a frightening and unmistakable sign of HAPE. If someone is suspected of having this serious illness, transport him or her to a lower elevation *immediately*, even if this requires traveling at night or during a storm. A descent of even a few thousand feet often brings dramatic results, unless the disease has progressed too far. Meanwhile, rangers should be contacted and plans made for evacuation.

Lightning is always a hazard in mountain country, and especially so the higher one goes. Ridges and summits must be avoided when thunderheads are roiling overhead. Do not take shelter in talus caves: the body may be perfectly positioned in the "spark gap." Squat, don't sit, if lightning is striking close by. Pray or curse, depending on your mood. And don't ever get in the same predicament again!

Some Sierra travelers always carry a compass; I have never done so and have never felt deprived. But a compass doesn't weigh much, and, in a severe storm with whiteouts, or in the few dense, trailless forests encountered, it could prove useful. Similarly, a global positioning satellite device could prove helpful on occasion, but one could argue that this gadget is a mere toy. Ditto with an altimeter watch. On the other hand, carrying a cellular phone could bring rescue in hours and thus save someone with HAPE. I will wager that in five years these will be seen in profusion. Many will abuse this instrument, calling for rescue for a sprained ankle; let us hope that such people will be charged the going rate for helicopters.

MAPS

The terrain covered by the High Route and its approaches is depicted superbly on various United States Geological Survey (USGS) quadrangles—or their privately published clones. Lately, however, a question has arisen: which of these maps to use? The superb 15-minute quads (with a scale of 1:62,500), in use from 1954 to the mid-1980s are now officially out of print, replaced by the far more detailed 7.5-minute series (with a scale of 1:24,000). This change might seem advantageous, but it really isn't, as far as the High Route is concerned. The new quads are far too detailed, for one thing. Every pond and hump is depicted—yet those who wish to identify a peak ten miles away may need to spread out three maps on the ground. Furthermore, it now takes twenty-one topos to show the entire High Route instead of eleven. And maps are expensive: the last leg of the journey, for instance, now requires four maps instead of two—and this costs about twenty-two dollars (in 1997).

The topo dilemma is partially solved in this book: twenty-four excerpts from the old 15-minute maps, covering the territory traversed by the High Route, have been included at the end of this book. (Since the High Route is not intended to be an actual trail, the course of the route is not shown.) Thus, it is not necessary to purchase the new 7.5-minute quadrangles, though it must be kept in mind that the various approaches to—and departures from—the High Route are rarely shown in full on the excerpts because of their small size. For this reason, I'd suggest that travelers supplement

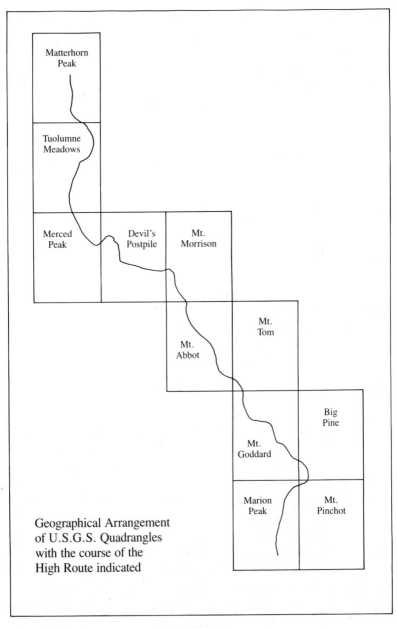

Matterhorn
Peak

Tuolumne
Meadows

Merced
Peak

Devil's
Postpile

Mt.
Morrison

Mt.
Abbot

Mt.
Tom

Big
Pine

Mt.
Goddard

Marion
Peak

Mt.
Pinchot

Geographical Arrangement
of U.S.G.S. Quadrangles
with the course of the
High Route indicated

these maps. Fortunately, there are several ways to do this.

The most useful maps for the High Route are, without question,
Tom Harrison's excellent 1:63,360 topo maps of various Sierra regions.

Four are needed for the High Route as far as Tuolumne Meadows: Kings Canyon, Mono Divide, Mammoth, and Yosemite. These colorful composites are formed from USGS topos and include mileages along established trails. For information and prices, call (800) 265-9090.

For the northernmost segment of the High Route (north of Tuolumne), the best overall map is the 1:63,360 topo map called Hoover Wilderness, published by the U.S. Forest Service.

Another possibility is to use the two huge sheets published by the

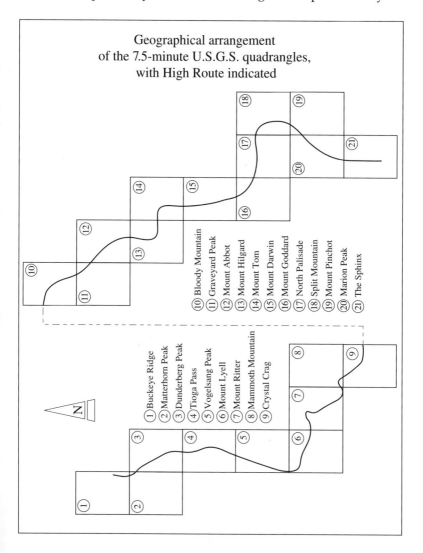

Geographical arrangement
of the 7.5-minute U.S.G.S. quadrangles,
with High Route indicated

① Buckeye Ridge
② Matterhorn Peak
③ Dunderberg Peak
④ Tioga Pass
⑤ Vogelsang Peak
⑥ Mount Lyell
⑦ Mount Ritter
⑧ Mammoth Mountain
⑨ Crystal Crag
⑩ Bloody Mountain
⑪ Graveyard Peak
⑫ Mount Abbot
⑬ Mount Hilgard
⑭ Mount Tom
⑮ Mount Darwin
⑯ Mount Goddard
⑰ North Palisade
⑱ Split Mountain
⑲ Mount Pinchot
⑳ Marion Peak
㉑ The Sphinx

U.S. Forest Service but based on the 15-minute USGS quadrangles. These two, known collectively as the John Muir Wilderness Back-country maps, cover the Kings Canyon to Mammoth region at a scale of 1:63,360. These maps are excellent but, at twelve square feet each, a bit unwieldy in the field. One can purchase these maps at ranger stations and visitor centers on the east side of the Sierra.

Topographic maps can be purchased in many sporting goods stores near the Sierra, as well as in ranger stations and visitor centers. Backpacking specialty shops in major California cities also offer a complete selection.

The U.S. Forest Service maps, while showing approach roads excellently, aren't of much use in the high country; they have no contour lines and not many place names.

Two accompanying diagrams indicate the names of the two sets of USGS quadrangles needed for the High Route and their geographic relationship to one another. The approximate course of the High Route has been added. Notice that not every map may be needed: sometimes the High Route traveler traverses a corner of a quad for only a very few miles.

Having two sets of quadrangles makes life miserable for a guide-book writer. Inconsistencies abound, even in the titles of maps: *Mt.* sometimes; *Mount* at other times. More seriously, elevations are often slightly different with the new surveys, and new names have sprung up. In this book I have used the awkward convention of putting new map information in parentheses when it seemed necessary to clarify a route description. For example: "From Lake 10,743 (10,798 on the Mt. Hilgard quad) ascend slabs . . . " Luckily, this problem isn't common. I have omitted this convention from the section called "Reversing the Route." I also don't bother to give the new elevations for features named on both maps—the height is largely irrelevant in such cases.

PERMITS

The Sierra Nevada, with more than thirty million people living within a day's drive, has experienced a population explosion in the past three decades. In August, dozens of backpackers cluster around the popular campsites deep in the mountains, and a continuous stream of hikers passes along the major trails. Although High Route trekkers will rarely encounter such scenes, they obviously must obey the rules and regulations established by the U.S. Forest Service and the National

Park Service in recent years to help preserve the wilderness. Most of these regulations are sensible and easy to obey. For instance, one must camp at least 100 feet away from water; forego campfires in many areas (for example, no fires above 10,000 feet in Kings Canyon National Park and none above 9,600 feet in Yosemite); and, in some fragile areas, avoid camping altogether.

The first thing to learn about regulations is that they change constantly. Don't believe what you read here, although this information was current as of late 2007. Several phone numbers are listed below, though they often change also! Smart hikers will call months ahead of their trip to avoid disappointments.

Foremost in importance among the regulations is the one that requires every party entering the High Sierra for an overnight stay to possess a wilderness permit. This can create potential problems for Sierra wanderers who plan a spur-of-the-moment trip during the most popular time of year. (A hiker caught without a permit, by the way, will be assessed a hefty fine and ordered to leave the mountains; rangers with radios regularly patrol the high country.)

Requests for permission to enter the High Sierra on virtually all trails from the east from May 1 to November 1 should be made months ahead of time if the traveler wishes to be *guaranteed* entry at a particular place and time. (Permits are also required for travel before and after this time frame, but these are automatically issued—no quotas apply.)

Here's how to do it. No earlier than six months before the desired date of entry, call Inyo National Forest in Bishop (760) 873-2538. Better still, use the Internet for current information.

Though Mount Whitney is not near the High Route, it should be mentioned that this extremely popular peak operates under a completely different set of restrictions and fees.

Hikers who haven't planned ahead aren't completely out of luck. If the quota for a given east-side trail is not fully booked in advance, hikers can pick up permits the day before the hike begins at a ranger station close to the trailhead. But popular passes like Piute, Bishop, and Mono are usually booked months ahead of time; those who choose the lesser-known entry points will stand a better chance. The spontaneous traveler must be flexible.

The above permit policy covers virtually the entire east flank of the range, from the Whitney area to barely north of Tioga Pass. High

Route hikers who begin in Kings Canyon, Tuolumne Meadows, or Twin Lakes are *not* affected by such draconian rules and can often get one of the many free, first come-first served permits on the day before their trip, or even on the actual day itself. One can also obtain a permit ahead of time for these entry points, and listed below are addresses and phone numbers. A permit request should include the same entry/exit/dates information given above.

For entry at Kings Canyon, the southern terminus of the High Route, write to Kings Canyon National Park, Three Rivers, CA 93271. Telephone: (559) 565-3766.

Hikers heading north from Tuolumne Meadows over the final portion of the High Route should contact the Yosemite Association, Box 545, Yosemite, CA 95389. Telephone: (209) 372-0740. Advance reservations cost five dollars per person.

Backpackers desiring to work their way south from Twin Lakes, the northern terminus of the High Route, should contact Wilderness Permit Applications, Bridgeport Ranger Station, Box 595, Bridgeport, CA 93517-0595. For information, telephone (760) 932-7070; permits, however, can be obtained only by mail. Advance reservations are five dollars per person and can be made beginning March 1. The cut-off date for advance permits is May 31, but call to confirm this date: it may change.

Other east-side ranger stations can provide information. The number for the Bishop station is (760) 873-2400. For Mammoth, call (760) 924-5500. For Lee Vining, call (760) 647-3044.

INTERNET

The Internet has hundreds of sites of interest to the High Sierra traveler. Search engines will lead one to current regulations, addresses, map resources, and much more for the national forests and parks mentioned in this book. Since this book was written, many changes have taken place regarding mandatory bear cannisters, campfire altitude limits, etc. The informed High Route traveler would do well to research these constantly evolving changes.

PLACE NAMES

Certain place names found in this guide do not appear on most maps, and the curious reader may wonder about their origins. Several of these names have been used in various guidebooks and have become fairly well known. Other names, bestowed decades ago, have faded into obscurity and are here resurrected. Some of the names are my own, invented especially for this book.

The following features were named by early Sierra pioneers and first appeared in print in the indicated annual issues of the *Sierra Club Bulletin*: Lake Frances (1905); Frozen Lake Pass (1923); Glacier Lake Pass (1938); Red Pass (1936); Snow-Tongue Pass (1905); White Pass (1936); and Windy Point (1936).

Guidebook writers often need to fabricate names in order to render complex terrain more understandable to their readers. The following features were named by unknown persons and initially appeared in print in the 1954 edition of *A Climber's Guide to the High Sierra*, published by the Sierra Club: Cirque Pass, Duck Pass, Feather Peak, Gabbot Pass, and Potluck Pass.

I invented the names Feather Pass and Horse Creek Pass for my 1976 version of the Sierra Club's revised guide, *The Climber's Guide to the High Sierra*.

Nancy Pass was named in the early 1970s by Don Scanlon in memory of his daughter.

The name Vennacher Col first appears in the 1974 edition of *High Sierra Hiking Guide to Mt. Pinchot*, published by Wilderness Press. The name Secret Lake appears in print for the first time in the same publisher's 1971 volume, *High Sierra Hiking Guide to Matterhorn Peak*.

The following names are solely my fabrications; applied mostly to passes, they either echo the name of an adjoining feature, commemorate some feature in proximity to a pass, or, as described in the text, refer to a significant historical event: Bear Lakes Basin, Bighorn Pass, Blue Lake Pass, Goat Crest Saddle, Grouse Lake Pass, Mine Shaft Pass, Puppet Pass, Shout-of-Relief Pass, Sky Pilot Col, Stanton Pass, Whitebark Pass, and White Bear Pass.

High Route hikers wishing to know the origin of hundreds of other Sierra place names should read Peter Browning's *Place Names of the Sierra Nevada* (1986).

RATING SYSTEM

Climbers long have used a rating system to differentiate the levels of difficulty encountered on a climb or its approach. Although such classifications rarely appear in this book, at times their use proves unavoidable. The following paragraphs briefly explain the system.

Class 1 indicates either trail walking or extremely easy cross-country travel.

The class 2 category—common along the High Route—means that the terrain has become more rugged. At all times hikers must watch where they plant their boots; hands must be used occasionally to maintain balance. Steep talus exemplifies this level of difficulty. Few hikers will have trouble on class 2 terrain.

Class 3 terrain is encountered on the northern side of a few High Route passes. Here, actual handholds and footholds must be found, tested, and used. The angle of the rock has steepened to the point where a fall might result in injury. The traveler must use caution while moving across this type of landscape, and inexperienced hikers should be aided in every possible way by persons more familiar with this scary terrain.

Class 4 terrain means that the holds have become smaller and the exposure has increased. A rope should be used to safeguard the climbers. In this book, only the optional ascent of Mount Humphreys falls into this category.

Chapter One

THE EXPLORERS

Something will be lost, no doubt, when many pilgrims follow the mountain trails—when this wilderness, like Switzerland, is smoothed and carved for the foot of man and dotted with lodges for his comfort. It must be, and on the whole it is best; but the facile tourists of the future will be less happy than we adventurers, who found nature virgin and inviolate, and braved her beauty and terror in the mood and manner of the pioneers.

—Harriet Monroe,
from the June 1909 issue of the *Sierra Club Bulletin*

The remarkable story of the pioneers who explored the timberline country of the High Sierra a century ago remains relatively unknown today. Books such as Hal Roth's *Pathway in the Sky: The Story of the John Muir Trail* (1965) and Francis Farquhar's *History of the Sierra Nevada* (also 1965) deal briefly with these early explorations, but Roth's lavishly illustrated volume focuses, as its subtitle implies, on the history of the trail itself, and Farquhar's comprehensive work deals with the exploration—and subsequent development—of the periphery of the High Sierra, a story that encompasses such events as the discovery of Yosemite Valley and the influx of that frenetic throng of gold-seekers known as the Forty-Niners. Shirley Sargent's biography of Theodore Solomons, *Solomons of the Sierra* (1989), is enticing, but her Sierra chapters are necessarily limited to the few summers her subject spent exploring the range. The most recent book to deal with the Range of Light is *The High Sierra: Wilderness of Light*

(1995), which contains magnificent photographs by Claude Fiddler and a brief historical overview (by me, massively condensed from the following section).

The following history relates the story of the high-country exploration in a far more comprehensive fashion than do the works cited above. My account is admittedly biased in favor of the published recollections of those pioneers most committed to locating a "high mountain route" between Yosemite Valley and Kings Canyon. Although I mention explorations of other significant regions of the High Sierra for the sake of completeness—such as the Mount Whitney massif—I emphasize the wanderings that took place north of Kings Canyon, in that immense wilderness where the Sierra High Route traverses ridges and basins for nearly 200 miles.

The articles and books written by the early explorers provide an exciting glimpse into an era when maps were either unavailable or inaccurate, trails were rudimentary, and travelers so few that when they encountered one another deep in the mountains, more often than not they would join forces for further exploration. These pioneers published dozens of lucid accounts of their journeys between 1863 and 1908, the most significant period of High Sierra exploration. After 1892, the year the Sierra Club was founded, many of these accounts appeared in that organization's well-respected journal, the *Sierra Club Bulletin.*

The men and women who described their travels during these years were educated and imaginative, eminently capable of capturing on paper the sense of wonder and euphoria they had experienced while tramping through the timberline country. But readers who peruse their accounts nowadays will be struck by a curious anomaly: sensitive though these writers were to their natural environment, they failed to convey any of their emotions beyond the most simple and predictable ones, such as joy at being in the mountains, or disappointment when stymied by an obstacle. True, these explorers were, for the most part, reserved, well-bred city dwellers who kept their personal lives inviolate. And, of course, the forgiving atmosphere of High Sierra travel—compared, for instance, to the stressful conditions found on an Arctic expedition—meant that strong emotions probably rarely surfaced. Still, if the early articles imply that such emotions as fear, anger, and boredom were totally absent, perhaps present-day readers can imagine, using their own trips as a basis, the reality of the day-to-day life of the pioneers. Indeed, one must conjure up these realities to avoid thinking of the early explorers as sober demigods striding like robots along preordained tracks.

WANDERERS

Little is known about the high-country ramblings of the first inhabitants of the Sierra Nevada, the Indians. Early on, the indigenous peoples discovered they could safely cross the highest parts of the range via several straightforward passes. The vast differences in ecology between the moist, forested western slope of the Sierra and its desertlike eastern flank meant that tribes such as the Miwoks and Yokuts, who lived on the western slope, coveted the specialties of the main east-side tribe, the Paiutes, and vice versa. Thus, using the high passes in summertime, the Indians living on the drier side of the range transported such goods as salt and pinyon-pine nuts westward, returning with, among other goods, beads made from seashells. Each tribe must have been pleased to find that the other would relinquish valuable commodities in exchange for common ones.

Whether or not the Indians ventured far from these trade routes remains unknown, but it's safe to assume that they rarely lingered in timberline country. Living far below this region, rarely above the 4,000-foot level, the tribes of the western slope were usually assured of plentiful game and relatively benign winters. The natives living beneath the precipitous eastern flank undoubtedly avoided the ultimate heights because of the awesome topography. Nevertheless, during lean periods, both groups must have pursued their prey as far as timberline, and, if a wounded animal struggled higher, even toward the summits: arrowheads have been discovered above 12,000 feet.

Although the Indians must have reached minor summits and remote lake basins on occasion, it is likely that both hunters and tradesmen felt relieved when descending from that lonely, rocky world where the sun burned and the chill winds howled. The indigenous people, then, probably knew relatively little of the region now traversed by the High Route, for there was no compelling reason for them to explore such an unproductive landscape.

During the late eighteenth century and the first decades of the nineteenth, the Spanish moved northward through California, establishing a string of twenty-one missions along the coastal region. They also settled in California's great central valley, and from this fertile plain they caught occasional glimpses of the high mountains to the east, bestowing upon them the prosaic name Sierra Nevada. Loosely translated, the name means a snowy, serrated range. While pursuing Indians, the Spanish made numerous forays into the foothills, but, satisfied that little of interest lay higher, they made no recorded attempt to reach the timberline country. Most of the largest rivers rushing from the heart of the range were named during the Spanish occupation, including the Merced, the San Joaquin, and the Kings. (The latter name is a shortened translation of the original: *El Río de los Santos Reyes.*)

Frémont's Adventures

In the mid-1840s Lieutenant John Frémont of the United States Army was sent west with instructions to fill in certain gaps on maps of the American West. On his first trip—guided by Indians and accompanied by scout Kit Carson—Frémont crossed the Sierra Nevada south of Lake Tahoe, discovering that marvelous body of water from a nearby peak.

On his second expedition, in 1845, the lieutenant surmounted the Sierra north of Tahoe and descended the range's western flank to the great central valley. In mid-December Frémont, sixteen men, and a herd of cattle set off down the immense valley, intending to join the remainder of the expedition, which had been instructed earlier to cross the range far to the south. Failing to make the rendezvous, Frémont turned east toward the high mountains, hoping to encounter his compatriots. As the new year approached, the expedition found itself near timberline, burdened with cattle and ill-equipped for the biting cold. As if to cap the misery, snow began to fall. Abandoning their cattle, the men fled to the lowlands and safety.

Although the exact location reached by Frémont on his historic trip will never be known—his description is ambiguous—the easternmost point attained by the lieutenant must have been somewhere in the timberline country near the headwaters of the North Fork of the Kings River. Despite worries about his men, Frémont seems to have enjoyed his brief sojourn, writing later that he had found the "exercise exhilarating."

In the years following the discovery of gold in the Sierra foothills in 1848, the Forty-Niners investigated every gulch and hillside in the Mother Lode country. Although the foothills were thus systematically explored, the miners paid scant attention to the less productive region high to the east.

The Surveyors

As late as 1860, ten years after California achieved statehood, little was known about the geography or resources of either the High Sierra or the other mountainous regions of the state. To rectify this situation the state legislature established the California Geological Survey that year. Soon called the Whitney Survey—after its leader, Josiah Whitney—this small band of professionals became the first to explore the timberline country officially. Since other areas of the state were deemed more important than the Sierra, not until 1863 did the group venture into the heart of the range. Yosemite Valley, that spectacular glacial canyon linking the foothills to the high mountains, was relatively well known by the 1860s, and Whitney, William Brewer, and Charles Hoffmann spent eight days there, mapping and marveling. In late June the three men climbed northward out of the valley toward little-known territory. On June 24 they ascended a prominent peak that was quickly named Mount Hoffmann in honor of the group's cartographer. This straightforward climb marked the first verified ascent of a major High Sierra peak and symbolizeed the beginning of an era that present-day mountaineers can only envy.

A few days later, from their camp near Tuolumne Meadows, Brewer and Hoffmann climbed a massive peak on the main Sierra crest. So impressed were they with the view that Brewer persuaded Whitney to climb it with him the following day. According to Brewer's journal, Whitney "thought the view the grandest he had ever beheld, although he has seen nearly the whole of Europe."

This ascent of Mount Dana, easy though it was, marked the end of Josiah Whitney's mountaineering career. Perhaps he became altitude sick, perhaps he felt he could direct the Survey better from the big cities; in any case, he soon departed for the lowlands, never again to return to timberline country. William Brewer, at age thirty-four, became the de facto leader of the Sierra contingent of the California Geological Survey.

Brewer and Hoffmann, entranced with the high peaks surrounding them, soon set off to the south, following the Tuolumne River toward a looming, snow-clad mountain they had spied from Mount Dana. Since they had christened this latter peak in honor of the most

prominent American geologist of that era, their next goal was named
Mount Lyell, after the most eminent British geologist of the time. Although the glaciated mass proved "inaccessible," according to Brewer,
the two men at least were able to survey a large section of new
territory.

During the journey toward Mount Lyell, the two men had dis-
cussed at length the course of the Civil War, finding humorous parallels between that conflict and the insect world: "Mosquitoes
swarmed in myriads, with not one-tenth the fear but with twice the
ferocity of a southern Secessionist," remarked Brewer. Defenders of
the Union, Brewer and Hoffmann had been distressed by the news
received at their camp in Tuolumne Meadows: General Lee had in-
vaded Pennsylvania with an army of 76,000 men. Only later did the
climbers learn that the Battle of Gettysburg had been raging during
the very hours they had spent just beneath Mount Lyell's summit, "at
least sixty miles from civilization on either side, among the grandest
chain of mountains in the United States."

The following year, 1864, marked the first recorded explorations
into the unknown heartland of the central and southern portions of
the High Sierra. Brewer, Hoffmann, Clarence King, James Gardiner,
and several packers entered the mountains in late June, south of the
great canyon of the South Fork of the Kings River. Within days, Brewer
and Hoffmann climbed a prominent, pyramidal peak; from the top
of this 13,570-foot mountain the two men were captivated by the apparently endless array of spires, canyons, and cirques to the east. Taking advantage of the bird's-eye view, Brewer named many of the most
prominent peaks, including one massive landform fourteen miles to
the southeast: Mount Whitney. This mountain, he felt, was surely the
range's loftiest point.

Back in camp, the two climbers of what soon was christened
Mount Brewer related the day's adventures to the others. The vision
of such high, unexplored peaks rising only a few miles away proved
too much for Clarence King to bear silently. The twenty-two-year-old
geologist, fresh from the Yale Scientific School, pleaded with Brewer
to let him attempt one of the huge peaks, preferably Whitney itself.
Brewer had taken note of the chaotic landscape lying between Brewer
and the Whitney massif; reluctantly, he gave his permission.

King and his companion, packer Richard Cotter, soon embarked
on an adventure now part of High Sierra folklore. Their five-day trek

Mount Whitney, with the Alabama Hills in the foreground

across absolutely uncharted terrain involved the most difficult and intricate cross-country travel ever done in North America up to that time. The present-day backpacker who follows their general route will be impressed with the rugged and convoluted country in proximity to the serrated divide that separates the Kings and Kern Rivers. Small cliffs continually block progress, and ledges that appear to lead to easier scrambling terminate over impassable dropoffs. Talus slopes prove to be steep and unstable, and treacherous snowfields linger throughout much of the summer. Nevertheless, the terrain that makes up the Kings-Kern Divide is by no means as intimidating as King implies in his embellished account recorded years later in *Mountaineering in the Sierra Nevada*. Most adventure writers of the late nineteenth century apparently felt their audiences would be impressed

only with sensational feats, and the journey related by King conse-
quently glows with drama and suspense. In one famous scene, Cotter, in the lead on a steep cliff, drops King a rope and informs him
that he can place his weight on it if he so desires. Thus reassured, King
decides it would be more sporting to climb the rock rather than the
rope. Upon reaching Cotter, however, he is shocked to see his companion perched precariously on a sloping ledge. King realizes that
they both could have fallen to their deaths had he actually tugged on
the rope. Greatly impressed with his comrade's courage, King wrote
that Cotter "might easily have cast loose that lasso and saved himself." King's rendition of their ascent of a high peak a few days later—
not Mount Whitney, but by mistake the closer and lower Mount
Tyndall—makes the reader wonder how both men survived.

Later in July, a group of prospectors who had crossed the range
from the east encountered Brewer's party and recommended a visit
to the nearby gorge formed by the South Fork of the Kings River. Now
world famous as Kings Canyon, this idyllic valley served as the
expedition's base camp for a week. In scouting the surrounding
countryside, members of the Survey climbed north to the Monarch
Divide, some 7,000 feet above the canyon floor. From this high ridge—
the divide between the South and Middle Forks of the Kings—the
group bestowed the names of their two heroes, King and Cotter, on
two conspicuous peaks to the east. To the north, far in the distance,
lay a spectacular, jagged ridge of dark peaks: the Palisades seemed
an appropriately descriptive name. To the northwest, eighteen miles
distant, rose an enormous, solitary pyramid that the men named in
honor of George Goddard, an early California surveyor. Present-day
adventurers who travel the High Route will reach the approximate
spot from which these great peaks were named, and, later on the journey, will pass so close to North Palisade and Mount Goddard that
their respective ascents will require only a few hours' detour.

Unable to discover a pack-animal route over the Monarch Divide
into the Middle Fork of the Kings, members of the Survey instead ascended east up Bubbs Creek, a major tributary of the South Fork. Following an old Indian trade route, the expedition crossed the range at
Kearsarge Pass and descended into Owens Valley, that vast trench
lying below the eastern escarpment of the southern Sierra Nevada.

The expedition members quickly completed a fifty-mile stretch
up Owens Valley and reentered the mountains at Mono Pass, another

ancient Indian route across the range. From a camp on Mono Creek, some ten miles west of the crest, Brewer, Hoffmann, Cotter, and a soldier named Spratt attempted to reach lofty Mount Goddard, then several days' journey to the south. Cotter and Spratt came within several hundred feet of reaching the top, retreating only because both daylight and food were running out. This epic trip, which traversed many miles of wild and unknown country, merited a few short paragraphs in Brewer's journal; had Clarence King been along, the adventure surely would have formed an entire chapter in his book.

Brewer was becoming restless at Mono Creek, as his journal entry for August 14 indicates: "Rides over almost impassable ways, cold nights, clear skies, rocks, high summits, grand views, laborious days, and finally, short provisions—the same old story." Thus, on the following day the group began a hurried march toward civilization, reaching Yosemite a week later. The partial exploration of the Mono Divide marked the final High Sierra adventure for Brewer, who shortly received a professorship at Yale, a position he was to hold for the next thirty-nine years. During his four years with the California Geological Survey, the scientist had traveled a remarkable 15,000 miles—half by horseback, 3,100 miles by foot, and the remainder by public conveyance.

Although the Survey was to remain active for another decade, its members rarely again ventured into the timberline country, and it is the expeditions of 1863 and 1864 that are the most significant in the early history of the High Sierra. In 1865 a well-illustrated volume describing the Survey's work up to that time was published. This report, concerned mainly with the state's geology, nevertheless indicated the general course of the major Sierra rivers, informed the reader that prominent peaks had been named and charted, and related, in prose far less flamboyant than Clarence King's, that a few peaks now had cairns on their summits. One peak that remained untouched, however, was Mount Whitney, by 1865 acknowledged to be the range's highest summit. The travails endured by King as he pursued this goal form one of the most beguiling chapters in Sierra history.

CLARENCE KING AND MOUNT WHITNEY

King's failure to climb the great peak in July 1864 had exasperated him, and immediately upon his return from Mount Tyndall he had begged his chief to let him try again. Brewer, knowing his assistant could fill in yet more blanks on the Survey's charts, gave the impatient youth a hundred dollars and an escort of two soldiers. This small expedition crossed the Kern River plateau and, after several days of needlessly complex maneuvering, finally set up camp beneath Mount Whitney. But King again failed to reach his goal, having inexplicably chosen the most difficult possible approach.

King's professional duties kept him in other regions of the United States until 1871, but in June of that year he detoured to Lone Pine, the village east of Mount Whitney, confident that he would not be rebuffed a third time. With a companion he managed to struggle upward to a prominent summit, but forbidding storm clouds blanketed the nearby peaks and rendered the view worthless. Although this meant that King could not confirm his success, he returned to his geological duties certain he had reached his goal at last. The word soon spread that the nation's highest peak had been conquered.

The emotions of the young geologist must have ranged from anger through disbelief to humiliation when, two years later, he read a scientific paper claiming he had reached a false Mount Whitney in 1871. The person who had written this disturbing piece recently had ascended King's mountain (later to be named Mount Langley) and had been astonished to see, only five miles to the north, a significantly higher peak. King hurriedly entrained for California and on September 19, 1873, finally stood atop the towering peak he first had glimpsed nine years earlier. But there he endured yet another disappointment, for a note in a pile of rocks indicated he was not the first to reach the summit plateau. One month earlier, three men from the Owens Valley, hearing of the controversy, had taken advantage of their on-the-spot location to solve forever the mystery surrounding the mountain. And so ended King's final adventure in the High Sierra. As historian Francis Farquhar noted, King was "far too cock-sure, far too impetuous, to be a good mountaineer." Regardless of his ineptitude—or perhaps because of it—Clarence King remains one of the most endearing characters ever to roam the high country.

PROSPECTORS, ADVENTURERS, AND HERDERS

Surveyors and miners were casual visitors to the High Sierra in the decades following King's misadventures. The Wheeler Survey, commissioned by the federal government, charted the rugged region north of Tuolumne Meadows during the late 1870s. Prospectors penetrated deep into the range, but, like the Indians, they preferred wooded valleys to alpine meadowlands. Only the hardiest miners plied their trade above timberline. Still, there can be little doubt that some of the summit cairns discovered by later travelers were constructed by these seekers of riches.

Other individuals curious to see or study the High Sierra also tramped through the range in the 1870s and 1880s, exploring new territory and making their findings public. The Kern River plateau, west of Mount Whitney, was investigated by three men with the alliterative last names of Wales, Wallace, and Wright; their names now grace lakes in the vicinity. Judge E. C. Winchell of Fresno spent several days in Kings Canyon, later penning a lengthy article for a San Francisco newspaper. The judge's son, Lilbourne, became, in 1879, the first person to stand atop Mount Goddard, the eminence that so dominates the central Sierra. Frank Dusy, a sheepherder, was apparently the first white man to stroll along the floor of the immense gorge of Tehipite Valley, just north of Kings Canyon.

Most famous among the adventurers of this era was naturalist John Muir. Arriving in the high country in the summer of 1868, the thirty-year-old Scot became an expert on the ecology of the High Sierra, formulating over a period of years his theory that glaciers were responsible for carving the U-shaped valleys so characteristic of the landscape. In addition to being a first-rate naturalist and writer, Muir was also a first-class climber. His ascent of Cathedral Peak in 1869 ranked as the most difficult climb yet accomplished in the United States. In the autumn of 1872 Muir guided a group of painters, including William Keith, to Tuolumne Meadows. Leaving his clients to work in this exceedingly lovely place, he set out alone toward the headwaters of the Middle Fork of the San Joaquin River. Lofty Mount Ritter was his goal, and he managed to reach its top successfully, though not without incident. Partway up a steep cliff, Muir found himself unable to move in any direction. Just as a fall seemed imminent, "life blazed forth again with preternatural clearness," as he wrote later in *The Mountains of California.* Soon he was moving gingerly upward toward the summit.

Little is known about the exact course of Muir's wanderings, for though he kept meticulous and eloquent notes of the natural scene, he rarely reported his itinerary. At some point in his travels he is known to have climbed a high peak near the head of the South Fork

Cathedral Peak

of the San Joaquin River. He was under the impression he had climbed mighty Mount Humphreys, but historian Francis Farquhar, by matching Muir's description with known landmarks, believed it was far more likely that the naturalist had ascended Mount Darwin.

Muir wrote an enormous amount about the Sierra, and some of his prose remains unsurpassed. Here's a sample from the August 1873 issue of *Overland Monthly:* "I drifted about from rock to rock, from stream to stream, from grove to grove. Where night found me, there I camped. When I discovered a new plant, I sat down beside it for a minute or a day, to make its acquaintance and hear what it had to tell. When I came to moraines, or ice-scratches upon the rocks, I traced them back, learning what I could of the glacier that made them. I asked the bowlders I met, whence they came and whither they are going. I followed to their fountains the traces of the various soils upon which the forests and meadows are planted; and when I discovered a mountain or rock of marked form and structure, I climbed about it, comparing it with its neighbors."

Of all the groups visiting the High Sierra during this era, none were so persistent as the sheepherders. The lush meadows liberally dotting the western flank of the range—from the foothills to timberline—provided excellent summer forage for their flocks. Enormous numbers of sheep roamed the High Sierra during the second half of the nineteenth century, overgrazing the meadows and causing untold erosional damage. The sheepmen, naturally, were not concerned with the ecology of the Sierra; as soon as one meadow was devastated, the men would lead the "hoofed locusts"—as Muir called them—to another, more remote pasturage. In this manner the herders explored much of the timberline country, establishing crude trails in every region.

The American sheepherders of this time appropriated the vast meadowlands well below timberline; this usurpation of the most desirable land meant that the Portuguese and French—the second-class shepherds—had to search elsewhere for pasturage. As a consequence, foreigners were the first to explore much of the highest countryside. In an 1896 article in *Overland Monthly*, Theodore Solomons, the father of the high mountain route, described the capabilities of these men: "The 'Portooge' can take his pack train, his mules or burros, over ground that baffles the mountaineering craft of the most experienced American herders, and the Frenchmen are said to show their heels to the Portuguese. These Basques, or 'Bascoes' as they are called, who drive their sheep into the very teeth of the Californian Alps, are perhaps the most skilful mountaineers in the world." (Solomons surely would have altered this last sentence had he recalled the well-known exploits of English climbers such as Mummery and Whymper.) Even though there is no record of a herder reaching a difficult summit, it seems quite likely that some of the men occasionally scrambled up remote, rocky peaks in order to seek out the perfect meadow.

As city-bred mountaineers began investigating the High Sierra in the 1890s, they naturally sought out the nearest herder for advice about the lay of the land. "He is a good guide," Solomons once wrote generically in the *Sierra Club Bulletin*, "but is nearly worthless in directing others. He will draw diagrams on the sooty bottom of the 'fry-pan,' which you must vow are lucid, though you know in your heart they are ridiculous. Moreover, the country immediately beyond the precise limits of his range is stranger to him than Afghanistan to a Bowery bootblack."

Heeding the advice of John Muir and the newly formed Sierra Club, the federal government began to oust sheepmen and their voracious flocks from national forests and parks, jurisdictions that by the 1890s covered much of the Sierra Nevada. Naturally, the herders resented this interference by outsiders. Detachments of cavalry eventually succeeded in ferreting the renegades out of the Yosemite high country. Many years later, after the destructive animals had disappeared from the timberline country, mountaineer Chester Versteeg could write of this controversial era from a detached perspective: "Possibly, in our resentment at the manner in which the sheepman exploited the Sierra to his own ends, we are prone to forget the debt we owe him for preserving Indian routes and establishing new trails."

THE VISION OF SOLOMONS

Few of the prospectors, adventurers, and sheepmen who roamed the Sierra during the last third of the nineteenth century displayed any enduring interest in the overall geography of the great mountain chain. Not since William Brewer's time had anyone seriously surveyed the central and southern portions of the Sierra. In the 1890s, however, a handful of curious adventurers independently decided to penetrate the range, discover its secrets, and announce the results to the world. The first of these pioneers to contemplate a major expedition into the unknown heart of the range was Theodore Seixas Solomons.

The boy of thirteen who gazed at the Sierra Nevada on a pristine spring day in 1884 was totally unaware that any human had ever set foot in the range. From his uncle's ranch near Fresno, young Solomons stared at the distant mountains, for the first time seeing them not merely as background objects, but as "the most beautiful and mysterious sight" he had ever beheld. The Holsteins grazing in the vast fields of alfalfa faded from the foreground, and he envisioned himself "in the immensity of that uplifted world, an atom moving along just below the white, crawling from one end to the other of that horizon of high enchantment." These sentences, written fifty-six years after the fact, are obviously a romanticized version of a youth's vision. Still, one would like to believe Solomons' claim that it was on this very day that he first imagined the "idea of a crest-parallel trail through the High Sierra."

It was not until 1892 that Solomons had enough money and time to set out on his quest for a high mountain route. With one companion, Sidney Peixotto, he journeyed to Lake Tahoe in mid-May. Their plan, Solomons wrote later, was "no less than the complete subjugation in a single season of the entire High Sierra." Even though the winter had been milder than usual, deep snowfields continually slowed the progress of the men and their two mules; they took six weeks to reach Yosemite Valley. There, by fortuitous coincidence, they encountered Joseph Nisbet LeConte, the twenty-two-year-old son of Joseph LeConte, the renowned geologist. (Twenty years earlier, the elder LeConte, along with John Muir, suggested that glaciation, not cataclysm, was responsible for canyons such as Yosemite Valley.) The younger LeConte, beginning a distinguished career as a professor of engineering at the University of California, was embarking on a series of trips—forty-four in all—into the highest and most remote sections of the range.

Solomons and Peixotto teamed up with LeConte for an excursion south toward Mount Ritter, that dark beacon that looms immediately southeast of the present Yosemite National Park boundary. Following in the footsteps of John Muir, the three youths climbed the peak from the east; it was only the third time its 13,157-foot summit had been reached. Pleased with this conquest, the trio returned to Yosemite Valley.

By the beginning of August, Solomons felt the time had come to further "subjugate the High Sierra." But LeConte had business in the city, and Peixotto had doubts about continuing south. Perhaps the view from Mount Ritter's summit had discouraged Peixotto; perhaps he was weary after eighty straight days in the wilderness. It seems unlikely that the cause of his hesitancy was that he thought the "season was late," the polite excuse Solomons gave in 1940. It was, in fact, the ideal time to travel in the High Sierra. Whatever the reason for Peixotto's defection, Solomons decided to push south with only a mule for company.

Heading south from Tuolumne Meadows along the same route he had traveled in late July, Solomons again climbed Mount Ritter, this time from the west. Fascinated by photography, the youth managed to transport a heavy and awkward 8x10 view camera all the way to the top, a feat that resulted in a set of alpine pictures that proved to be the first high-quality photographs ever taken of the High Sierra.

The wide, forested valley of the Middle Fork of the San Joaquin River beckoned next, so Solomons broke camp and headed downstream to Devil's Postpile, a geological curiosity previously known only to local miners and sheepmen. After skirting the southern ramparts of the Ritter Range, Solomons curved west, reaching civilization in early September.

During the course of his 1892 trip, Solomons either crossed or saw all three of the major forks of the San Joaquin River. He had camped at the headwaters of the Middle Fork; from Mount Ritter's summit he had gazed straight down upon the source of the North Fork. But of the South Fork—the High Sierra's longest river—he had obtained only an enticing glimpse. Solomons realized that this major watercourse likely sprang from a great cluster of peaks thirty miles to the south. The vision of this unexplored landscape haunted him for the two years that passed before he was able to return.

The 1894 expedition undertaken by Solomons and nineteen-year-old Leigh Bierce—son of author Ambrose Bierce—was something of a disappointment in that the two men failed in their principal objective: to reach the famed gorge of Kings Canyon via a route close to the Sierra crest. "Such a high mountain route," Solomons wrote in 1895, "practicable for animals, between the two greatest gorges in the Sierra, has never been found—nor, indeed, sought—so far as my researches have revealed." Yet the visionary was confident not only that such a route existed but that it "would be a journey fit for the gods." He further predicted that "as a scenic mountain tour, I doubt if the world affords its like."

Instead of heading directly for the South Fork of the San Joaquin River—their avowed goal—Solomons and Bierce lingered in Yosemite, exploring and photographing the high country. It was not until mid-September that the two men, along with three pack animals, began ascending the South Fork toward the Sierra crest. Warned by sheepherders of the hazards accompanying autumn storms, the small expedition nevertheless worked far up the river, eventually curving east up Mono Creek, a major tributary. Soon the men reached a lovely valley, which Solomons named Vermilion Valley because of the color of its soil. Almost exactly thirty years earlier, William Brewer and his comrades had attempted Mount Goddard from this idyllic place. (In the mid-1950s the valley became Lake Thomas A. Edison, courtesy of the Southern California Edison Company.)

Solomons and Bierce next crossed into the Bear Creek watershed, following this turbulent stream first east, then south as it snaked toward its source. It was September 20 when they reached the base of an isolated peak christened Seven Gables because of its eccentric shape. That afternoon the pair ascended the 13,075-foot mass and from its top stared in awe at the panorama. A multitude of peaks, mostly unclimbed and unnamed, rose in every quadrant. Immediately to the east lay a cluster of towering summits, below which nestled dozens of jewellike lakes. The two men were quite probably the first humans ever to peer down into the wild set of cirques known today as the Bear Lakes Basin, one of the most striking landscapes traversed by the High Route.

Spectacular though the terrain was, Solomons knew they had reached an impasse, for their impending route, visible for the first time, looked feasible only to "mythological beasts with wings," as he wrote later in the *Sierra Club Bulletin*. Solomons soon conceived a bold plan: they would leave their pack animals with a sheepherder recently met downstream and set off south with fifty pounds each on their backs.

Before this plan could be effected, a major storm intervened, depositing several feet of snow. "We were on top of the Sierra," Solomons wrote, "some seventy-five miles of nearly waist-deep snow between us and the nearest settlements." It was obviously time for retreat. Unfortunately, the deep snow meant trail's end for the two remaining animals (the third had broken its leg and had been shot). One mule had strayed; it would either freeze or starve in the coming weeks. After shooting the other beast, the men hurried downstream. In the shambles of their camp lay the still-warm mule, Solomons' giant camera, all his exposed negatives, and quantities of waterlogged bedding. Days passed as the exhausted pair retraced their route downstream; finally, on the fifth day, they stumbled upon a stranded herder who plied them with mutton. Their 1894 expedition came to an end shortly thereafter.

Apparently undeterred by this experience, Solomons returned the following year, this time with Ernest Bonner. (Solomons never traveled with the same person twice, a fact that may have several possible interpretations.) With fresh memories of the previous autumn, the obsessed twenty-three-year-old made sure to arrive in the mountains early. Ignoring Yosemite this time, the two men arrived at the site of the former camp below Seven Gables in late June 1895. During the following two weeks, while waiting for the snowpack to diminish, Solomons systematically explored the surrounding countryside, leaving Bonner to tend camp and their one pack animal. Exactly where Solomons wandered during this period will never be known, for his notes, donated to the Sierra Club Library in San Francisco, were destroyed in the 1906 earthquake and fire. It seems likely that he would have ascended into nearby Bear Lakes Basin while searching for a passable route to the south; perhaps he even visited Feather Pass.

It *is* known that Solomons spent four days exploring the headwaters region of Mono Creek, and his photograph of the Mills Creek Lakes and Gabbot Pass, published in the May 1896 issue of *Overland Monthly*, indicates that he ascended Peak 12,691, a landmark on the ridge between the Second Recess and Third Recess. (These great U-shaped valleys—there are four—were called "magnificent alpine recesses" by Solomons in his article; thus place names are born.)

Solomons was now, more than ever, aware that rugged mountain travel could be accomplished far more effectively without pack animals. With this in mind, he and Bonner worked their way down to Jackass Meadow, on the South Fork of the San Joaquin River. Leaving their mule with a sheepherder on July 12, they began following the river south into new territory. The journey of the next two weeks ranks equally in Sierra history with the King-Cotter adventure of 1864. Solomons' accounts of this trip, published in various magazines and journals, are by no means as overblown as Kings'; indeed, his readable prose is eminently believable, and his enthusiasm for the High Sierra radiates from every page.

On July 14 the two explorers cached most of their equipment at the junction of the South Fork with the major tributary now known as Evolution Creek. Working their way up this stream, they soon emerged into an enchanting valley, where for three miles they strolled through pine forests interrupted by enormous meadows. Above what is now Evolution Valley—the "fairest paradise" Solomons had ever seen—the two men clambered up alongside innumerable cascades that raced down vast granite slabs. Reaching timberline at last, they beheld "a fine sheet of water," Evolution Lake. So impressed was Solomons with the magnificent scenery that he promptly bestowed names on nearly every peak in sight. These names, honoring philosophers and scientists prominent in the new field of evolution studies, included Mounts Darwin, Spencer, Huxley, and Fiske.

From their camp near Sapphire Lake, the two men climbed a prominent peak, quickly named Mount Wallace, on the crest to the east. From the summit they could see that Mount Darwin was the region's highest peak, and later that same day they made a bold dash for it, failing several hundred feet below the top when steep cliffs loomed. "Farther ascent," the usually rational Solomons wrote later, "is barred to all human beings."

On the following day Solomons and Bonner reluctantly departed the Evolution country, returned to their cache on the South Fork of the San Joaquin, and started south up the river. On July 19 they reached its source, the goal Solomons had been pursuing for three summers. Here, in an austere world of rock and snow, Solomons stood mesmerized by the looming black crags that surrounded him. Foremost among the peaks was Mount Goddard, the solitary monolith named by William Brewer's group thirty-one years earlier.

Solomons, of course, knew he wasn't the first person to stand in the shadow of the great peak. He had seen evidence of sheep not far down the canyon. He knew, too, that Cotter and Spratt must have passed the headwaters on their 1864 attempt, and he realized John Muir had been somewhere in the area in 1873. Finally, Solomons was quite aware that Mount Goddard had been climbed in 1879 by Lil Winchell and Louis Davis. Nevertheless, it was a striking landscape, and Solomons must have been extremely pleased to have completed this segment of his dream route.

The next morning proved even more awe-inspiring, for the pair climbed the 13,568-foot Mount Goddard, obtaining the finest view they ever had seen in the Sierra. Virtually every major peak in the range, from Mount Conness to Mount Whitney—a distance of 110 miles—was etched against the cobalt sky. Four hours passed as the two men absorbed the view, oblivious to an approaching storm. Rain poured down upon them as they stumbled down the steep talus. At 12,000 feet they reached the highest pines and stopped for the night.

"We had no sooner built a fire," Solomons wrote later, "than the snow began to fall, and though for a time it was nip and tuck between the two elements, our pitch-saturated logs conquered at last."

In the dawn light the two men began traversing east through what is now the Ionian Basin. Their immediate goal was a pass Solomons had spied earlier from the vicinity of Evolution Lake. If they could reach this broad saddle—now called Muir Pass—Solomons felt certain they could then descend into the headwaters region of the Middle Fork of the Kings River. But the storm's intensity increased, thwarting these plans. After struggling across slippery talus for several hours, Solomons resolved to flee the inhospitable alpine world and drop south into a deep gorge he had noticed from Mount Goddard's summit. Passing between two guardian peaks—immediately named Scylla and Charybdis—the adventurers began their descent. Acres of enormous boulders blocked the canyon floor, making their progress painfully tedious. In the rain, the slate forming the canyon walls shone like lustrous metallic plates. This narrow canyon—both sinister and beautiful—was named the Enchanted Gorge. (So remote is this feature that only three more parties were to pass through it during the next half-century.)

It was midafternoon on the following day when Solomons and Bonner emerged from the confining canyon into the flat meadowlands bordering the Middle Fork of the Kings River, having made a bonejarring descent of 7,600 feet in only two days. They had crossed the divide separating the San Joaquin watershed from the Kings drainage by about the most difficult possible route. The remainder of the trip from Simpson Meadow, on the Middle Fork, to Kings Canyon, on the South Fork, was anticlimactic, for a well-established trail led across the Monarch Divide.

Solomons realized that pack animals could not be taken through the Enchanted Gorge, and since his ambition had always been to discover a crest-parallel route negotiable to stock, he was back in the mountains the following summer. His companions in 1896 were two teenaged students from the University of California: Walter Starr and Allen Chickering. The three men, along with four horses, left Yosemite Valley on July 3. In mid-July, however, Solomons became ill and decided to leave the expedition near Jackass Meadow. The other two men, evidently not as obsessed as Solomons with a *high* mountain route, continued south through the forested country far to the west of Mount Goddard. Reaching Kings Canyon on August 3, the pair became the first party ever to travel continuously with pack animals from Yosemite to Kings Canyon. Although this was a praiseworthy accomplishment, they had traveled almost exclusively in the lowlands, far from the Sierra crest.

Solomons was not destined to return to the watershed of the Kings River. Perhaps he finally became discouraged with furthering his high mountain route; in his later writings he does not mention his reasons for abandoning his quest when it was but halfway accomplished. In 1897, instead of pushing south into the Kings River headwaters, as one might have expected, he "made improvements in the northern part of the route." It's possible that only the San Joaquin drainage truly fascinated him; certainly his name will be linked forever to this immense wilderness. During his five journeys between 1892 and 1897, Solomons bestowed approximately 100 place names, about 60 of which remain today. A short time after these Sierra trips, he moved to Alaska (and, a decade later, back to San Francisco), revisiting the upper San Joaquin watershed only once again, in 1932—at age sixty-two. In 1933 he wrote that he had departed the Sierra in 1897 assured about the completion of his high mountain route: "As for the Kings River section . . . I knew that with LeConte, Bolton Coit Brown and one or two other indefatigable ones, it was in safe hands."

BOLTON COIT BROWN AND THE KINGS RIVER WATERSHED

If Solomons had been obsessed with the San Joaquin drainage, Bolton Coit Brown was convinced that the Kings River watershed afforded the finest Sierra adventures. A professor of fine arts at Stanford University, Brown made three memorable visits to this area between 1895 and 1899. Unlike Solomons, he displayed little interest in a continuous Sierra high route, preferring instead to concentrate his energies in only one region. Using Kings Canyon and nearby Paradise Valley as his base camps, Brown thoroughly investigated the rugged country surrounding the headwaters of the South Fork of the Kings River.

The professor's 1895 trip to Arrow Peak remains a classic of solo exploration. Leaving Kings Canyon with one mule in late July, Brown trudged up the well-worn path leading over the Monarch Divide toward the Middle Fork. It seems entirely possible that along the way he encountered Solomons and Bonner, enervated from their descent of the Enchanted Gorge. If this meeting took place—both Brown and

Solomons independently write of traveling this segment in late July—
no record exists. But one can almost picture the trailside conversation.
Solomons, intensely pleased with his pioneering efforts, may well
have crowed a bit as he bestowed advice on newcomer Brown. Ironi-
cally, Solomons could not have known he was completing his last significant High Sierra exploration as he spoke to his unknowing heir
for the first and perhaps last time.

After spending several days exploring the great canyon of the
Middle Fork of the Kings, Brown began working up Cartridge Creek.
This major tributary of the Kings climbs steeply east toward Cirque
Crest, a northeasterly extension of the Monarch Divide. Leaving the
heavily forested valley behind, the professor and his mule reached
timberline country near Marion Lake. Shortly after passing this pleasant body of water, Brown was astonished to see a human bounding
down the hillside. It was a French sheepherder, complete with dog
and flock; the man indicated to Brown that the wide gap just to the
south was passable to stock.

On the following morning Brown ascended to what is now Cartridge Pass. Scrambling from the saddle up to the summit of nearby
Mount Ruskin, the professor looked straight down into Upper Basin,
the source of the South Fork of the Kings River. He counted twenty-six
sparkling lakes scattered over hundreds of square miles of pristine
wilderness. To the east, across Upper Basin, rose the impressive ramparts comprising the crest of the Sierra. Among these peaks was one
with a conspicuous gap on its broad summit; Brown named it Split
Mountain. A striking symmetrical peak to the south was christened
Arrow Peak. (A short time later, the professor wrote an essay dealing
with the naming of mountains. In it he chastises Solomons indirectly
by decrying persons who name mountains in honor of people, especially "men eminent in the physical sciences." Names such as Bridal
Veil and Devil's Slide also earned his ire: "All such pseudoromantic
appellations smack of childishness and of cheap sentimentalism.")

From his camp on the South Fork of the Kings River, Brown stared
with uncertain emotions at the classically shaped ridges rising to the
summit of the newly named Arrow Peak. The professor was in a quan-
dary. He was low on food and his shoes were in tatters; he obviously
should return as soon as possible to Kings Canyon. Yet, he wrote later,
the peak "called to me at breakfast, its rocky pinnacles beckoned
me, its soaring summit challenged me. I could stand it no longer

and hurriedly swallowing the last of my coffee, I threw prudence to the winds . . . and was away through the pines and the boulders, over the roaring stream . . . almost on the run for the sheer joy of that mountain." Possessing such a positive attitude, he was, of course, successful; from the summit his artist's eye spotted thirty-two lakes.

During the next few days Brown worked his way down the South Fork, knowing it would take him directly into Kings Canyon. But the terrain was rough, with brush and talus denying easy progress. At last Brown's mule became lame and could go no farther. Shouldering an enormous pack, the professor set off down the wild, white-walled canyon known today as the Muro Blanco. He soon returned to civilization, "shockingly ragged and sunburned and dusty."

In the summer of 1896 Brown and his bride, Lucy, spent a month and a half exploring the Bubbs Creek watershed and the region to its south. After climbing for several weeks in the environs of Bullfrog

Upper Basin and Split Mountain from Frozen Lake Pass

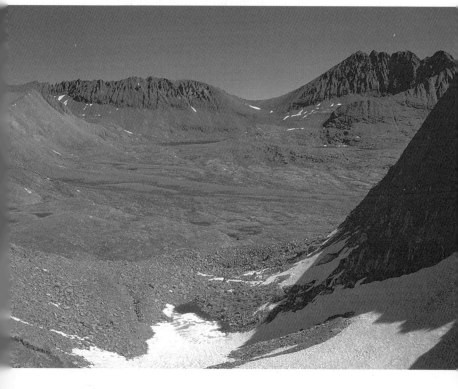

Lake, the honeymooners crossed the Kings-Kern Divide at an obvi-
ous low point near the notch negotiated thirty-two years earlier by
Clarence King and Richard Cotter. Brown was quite likely the first
person to speculate in print about the accuracy of King's account: "I
am strongly inclined to suspect that there was a general tendency with
Mr. King to put down the things he did not himself do as impossible.
His book is very far from giving a true impression of the region from
Brewer to Tyndall."

Lucy Brown proved to be as tough a mountaineer as her husband,
judging from the following one-day exploit. Arising from a wet bivouac, where they had dozed fitfully, the pair left their timberline camp
at the headwaters of the Kern River and headed east, intending to try
Mount Williamson. Not knowing its exact location, they mistakenly
started up a spur of the Kings-Kern Divide. Soon the couple recognized Williamson, some five miles to the east. They abandoned the
spur, sped across the tundra of Tyndall Creek Basin, and by noon
stood atop California's second-highest peak. Retracing their steps
nearly to their bivouac site, the Browns then turned north, crossed
Harrison Pass at sunset, and stumbled down 3,500 feet to their main
camp at East Lake. During this fifteen-hour odyssey, the professor and
his wife had tramped across twenty miles of rough cross-country terrain, coped with an elevation gain of 5,000 feet, and descended approximately 7,000 feet. The next day the newlyweds easily managed
the fourteen-mile jaunt back to Kings Canyon.

Later in the summer of 1896 Brown managed yet another remarkable feat, this one alone. A year earlier he had attempted the unclimbed Mount Clarence King, failing only a few hundred feet below
the summit. Now he was anxious to try the striking horn of granite
once again. During the course of one long day, Brown made the first
ascent of the peak from his camp in Paradise Valley. But it was neither the elevation gain of 6,300 feet nor the distance of twelve miles
that was especially noteworthy. What made this ascent so significant
was the difficulty of the upper section, for the summit, composed of
gigantic blocks and slabs, is sheer on some facets and merely steep on
the others. Brown carefully squirmed up intricate passages until finally, 100 feet below the top, he came to an apparent impasse. Tying a
knot in the end of a piece of rope, the professor cast it upward repeatedly until the knot lodged in a crack. Using the rope for assistance,
he inched higher. He performed this clever and unusual technique

several more times before reaching "the ugliest place of all," the summit block itself. There he tossed a short loop of rope over a rounded projection directly above his head and slowly shifted his weight onto the loop. It held, and he levered onto the summit, completing the most difficult North American rock climb of the nineteenth century. (Today his route is rated 5.4, meaning that ropes and protection should be used.) The view was spectacular and the exposure frightening. Imagining the consequences of a slip, Brown later wrote in the same vein as the man for whom the peak was named: "If you fall off one side, you will be killed in the vicinity; if you fall off any of the other sides, you will be pulverized in the remote nadir beneath."

Three years went by before Brown returned to the Kings River drainage. This time he was accompanied not only by Lucy, but by their two-year-old, Eleanor. The family spent most of their vacation investigating the beautiful lake basins east of Mount Clarence King. At some juncture, Brown relaxed his strictures on never naming features after people, for the largest Rae Lake appears on his published map as Lake Lucy and its most prominent isle as Eleanor's Island. Oddly enough, however, not one of the place names the professor bestowed in this area ever became official, in marked contrast to the features christened by Theodore Solomons.

Following his trip of 1899, Brown seems to have abandoned the High Sierra. His well-written articles, so prominent in the early issues of the *Sierra Club Bulletin,* ceased in 1901.

LeConte, the Chronicler

The late 1890s mark the emergence of yet another noted Sierra explorer, Joseph Nisbet LeConte, whose informative articles, maps, and photographs were to grace the *Bulletin* regularly for the next forty years. (For the remainder of this book, the name LeConte, unless otherwise stated, refers to this adventurer—not his father, also Joseph.)

As mentioned earlier, LeConte had accompanied Theodore Solomons and Sidney Peixotto on a trip to Mount Ritter's summit in 1892. During the next few years, "Little Joe" LeConte (he wasn't much above five feet in height) journeyed to the High Sierra several more times, concentrating his efforts in two locales: Yosemite National Park and the Kings Canyon area. In the course of these adventures, the young professor created a set of photographs so excellent that in 1944 Ansel Adams was to praise their quality and aesthetic values:

"His photographs are not the fruit of intellectual cogitations; they are the natural, inevitable selections of a man very much in tune with the world about him."

Early on, LeConte also became fascinated with the idea of mapping the high country, and to this end he obtained information from Solomons, Brown, and others, in addition to acquiring first-hand data. In 1893 the Sierra Club published his initial efforts—maps of the Yosemite and Kings Canyon regions. These maps, revised at intervals as new information became available, were greatly appreciated by the members of the newly established mountaineering and conservation organization; this reception unquestionably spurred LeConte to broaden his knowledge of the range.

LeConte's first significant mountaineering venture outside his familiar haunts came in 1898, when he and Clarence Cory decided to explore the possibility of a true high mountain route between Yosemite and Kings Canyon. During the early part of their month-long journey, the two men closely followed the pioneering route of their predecessor, Theodore Solomons, even to the extent of visiting the upper reaches of Mono Creek. From a camp near the junction of this stream and the Second Recess, the pair made the first ascent of Red Slate Mountain, the towering sentinel of this part of the Sierra. A few days later, from the top of Seven Gables, they were awestruck by the sight of unclimbed Mount Humphreys, a solitary monolith nine miles to the east. At that moment the men resolved to try for its tapered summit.

LeConte and Cory attempted to lead their pack animals toward the huge peak, but, finding no practical route, they returned to Blaney Meadows, a lush parkland on the South Fork of the San Joaquin River. Leaving their stock behind, the pair knapsacked into Humphreys Basin, a wild and austere region dotted with dozens of rockbound lakes. On July 7 they made their bid for the summit. After several false starts on various ridges, the men finally reached a small prominence on the mountain's northwest ridge, 500 feet below the top. The view upward was discouraging, as evidenced by LeConte's later description: "I have never felt so impressed, so utterly overpowered, by the presence of a great mountain as when standing amongst the crags of Mt. Humphreys looking up that smooth wall to its airy summit, and again down ten thousand feet into the depths of the Owen's Valley." So intimidated were the two men that they fled down the mountainside without even attempting the summit pinnacle. The immense landmark of the central Sierra would remain unascended for several more years.

Kings Canyon beckoned, so the two young men returned to their pack animals and began ascending toward the source of the South Fork of the San Joaquin. But upon climbing Mount Goddard they suffered a major disappointment, for they saw that it was impossible to lead their stock across the rugged divide anywhere near the great peak. Luckily, they recalled that sheepherders had mentioned a pack-animal route that circumvented the divide by means of the basins at the headwaters of the North Fork of the Kings River, not far to the west. Back down the San Joaquin the two men went, searching for a way across the ridge known today as the LeConte Divide. Discovering a passable route at last, the expedition soon reached the forested country visited by John Frémont and his men a half-century earlier.

A week later LeConte and Cory attained their goal, thus accomplishing the second complete journey between Yosemite and Kings Canyon. For a short distance they had traveled closer to the main crest than had their predecessors, Starr and Chickering; nevertheless, no one yet had traversed the southern Sierra close to the headwaters of the Middle and South Forks of the Kings River. The six-mile-long barrier known as the Goddard Divide, stretching from the LeConte Divide to the main crest, had forced all travelers into the less rugged country to the west. LeConte was to experiment with this crossing again, but not immediately, for he had long been fascinated by distant views of the Palisades, that serrated ridge named by Brewer's survey group. The next few summers, he decided, would prove rewarding if spent in this remote region.

As his first goal, LeConte chose the massive southern outrider of the Palisades, Split Mountain. Traveling the by-now familiar route from Kings Canyon, across the Monarch Divide, to the Middle Fork of the Kings, LeConte and his wife camped at lovely Simpson Meadow for a few days, savoring the scenery and the trout. On July 18, 1902, the couple and Curtis Lindley ascended alongside the Middle Fork until reaching Cartridge Creek; from this confluence they followed Bolton Coit Brown's 1895 route to Marion Lake—named on this 1902 trip by LeConte in honor of his wife of one year, Helen Marion Gompertz LeConte.

From the vicinity of Marion Lake the trio explored potential routes across the notched ridge separating them from Upper Basin, the source of the South Fork of the Kings. None of the notches reached on July 23 proved passable on their eastern sides, but on the following morning the undaunted threesome shouldered their packs and set off to reconnoiter the passes missed the previous day. Just when the venture seemed doomed, LeConte discovered what is now called Frozen Lake Pass, which, he later claimed in his article in the *Sierra Club Bulletin*, was "the only point where the Cartridge Creek Divide can be crossed." Beyond the 12,400-foot saddle lay Upper Basin, covered with tarns and tundra.

The next morning's climb of Split Mountain was somewhat anti-climactic, for the mountain proved to be one of the easiest LeConte ever had climbed. As usual, though, the view was spectacular, and he marveled at the complexity of the terrain in the same article: "For eighteen miles to the south, and eighteen miles to the north not a single one of the countless giants of the Main Crest has ever been climbed. We were in the heart of the High Sierra." The Palisades loomed to the northwest, but LeConte realized that their provisions had nearly run out; the dark cluster of summits so dominating the skyline would remain untouched for the time being. From their camp at Marion Lake, however, LeConte and Lindley dashed to the north to reach a mountain appropriately christened Observation Peak. From this vantage point the highest crags of the Palisades rose in full view, only five miles distant. LeConte mapped the area as best he could and vowed to return the following year.

Although the Palisades remained the last major uncharted region of the High Sierra, LeConte knew that the periphery of the group had been explored by sheepherders and prospectors. Bishop Pass, immediately north of the highest summits, was a known sheep route across the Sierra crest. Dusy Basin, that intriguing melange of water, stone, and pine just west of the pass, had been investigated in 1877 by Frank Dusy, a peripatetic sheepherder. Two years later, Lil Winchell, on his journey toward unclimbed Mount Goddard, passed close enough to the Palisades to name two of them. Later still, Theodore Solomons had viewed the jagged peaks from the top of Mount Goddard, and in an article for *Overland Monthly* he lavished excessive praise on the group: "The Palisade country, I have reason to believe, is the acme of alpine sublimity on the American continent." Of the jutting peaks themselves, however, absolutely nothing was known except their outlines and approximate elevation: 14,000 feet.

LeConte was determined to investigate the Palisades at closer range. In July 1903, James Hutchinson, James Moffitt, John Pike, Robert Pike, and the two LeContes retraced the previous year's route as far as Marion Lake. Leaving Helen LeConte and John Pike to tend camp, the four others struck north. Skirting Observation Peak on its east flank, the group dropped nearly 3,000 feet to an idyllic glade at the 8,800-foot level of Palisade Creek. This place, according to LeConte, was "absolutely untouched. Not since the creation of the forest reserve [in 1893] had human foot trod this glorious wilderness, and even before that time the sheepmen who visited the valley must have been few indeed, for not a blaze, monument, nor corral did we see, and there were but few signs of old sheep-camps."

That night's camp was established at timberline on Glacier Creek, not far below the mysterious peaks. Early on July 24 the men left camp and continued up the stream, traversing meadows, talus, and finally snowfields. Here they encountered acres of suncups, a phenomenon familiar to all who venture into the subalpine world. LeConte described them succinctly: "The unequal melting of the snow cut the whole mass up into a labyrinth of great knife-blades, which were sometimes four feet high and two or three feet apart. We were forced to step from blade to blade, balancing on the sharp edges, and often falling into the spaces between."

In spite of these obstacles, the well-conditioned men soon reached the main Sierra crest, astonished to see, immediately below them, the largest glacier in the range, complete with crevasses and a mile-long bergschrund. Greatly impressed with this unexpected sight, they turned toward the highest peak—North Palisade—and gasped. The jagged, half-mile ridge leading over to its summit appeared impossible. Hutchinson carefully traversed to the brink of a huge gash—now called the U-Notch—and verified the prognosis. The disappointed men scrambled up a consolation prize to the east: Mount Sill, a massive peak that LeConte had seen, and named, seven years earlier. To LeConte, the view from this 14,162-foot summit was "unparalleled in grandeur and extent." But there was no question in anyone's mind that the view was flawed in one respect: the image of nearby North Palisade, eighty feet higher and still virgin.

The next morning, unwilling to abandon their primary objective without at least one serious effort, LeConte, Hutchinson, and Moffitt

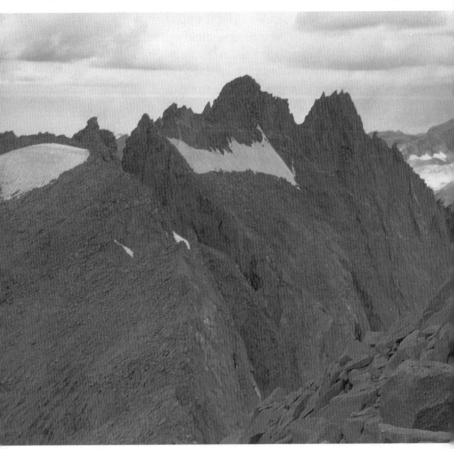

North Palisade from the top of Mount Sill

set off from camp once again. From what is now Potluck Pass—
reached by the present High Route—they gained an excellent view
of North Palisade's 1,500-foot-high southwest face, an imposing escarpment riven by steep chutes. Choosing the most prominent of
these, the three climbers worked up it until stymied by steepening
cliffs. Since these appeared unclimbable, it seemed the group must
fail once again. But as LeConte peered down the chute they had
just ascended, he spied a narrow ledge snaking around a corner.
This proved to be the key to the ascent, for the sloping shelf led to an
easier chute, which eventually ended near the summit. The highest
of the Palisades had been vanquished, and the geography of yet
another remote part of the High Sierra was better understood.

With the three highest summits of the Palisades conquered, LeConte returned to the Evolution country during the summer of 1904, accompanied this time by the eminent geologist Grove Karl Gilbert. The object of their journey—to travel from Yosemite to Kings Canyon as close to the Sierra crest as possible—was identical to that of LeConte's trip of 1898. But this time LeConte vowed to find a route for animals across the Goddard Divide.

On July 18, while sixty-one-year-old Gilbert studied the rocks of the Evolution region, LeConte followed Evolution Creek as it curved toward its source. The terrain proved remarkably gentle as far as the top of the Goddard Divide, but there, at what is the present-day Muir Pass, he stared down in dismay at "the savage black gorges of the Middle Fork region." This sobering sight convinced LeConte that stock could not be taken across the divide; furthermore, he saw no signs of sheep, another indication of the terrain's roughness. Soon the discouraged men tramped west and crossed the LeConte Divide at a notch slightly south of the one crossed by LeConte and Cory six years earlier. The new notch became Hell-for-Sure Pass, surely one of the most evocative place names in the High Sierra. A week later the expedition reached Kings Canyon, their fine trip marred only by their failure to cross the Goddard Divide.

HUTCHINSON, THE MOUNTAINEER

James Hutchinson, pleased with his ascents in the Palisades the previous year, was also active during the summer of 1904. The San Francisco attorney was the preeminent climber of the Sierra during the early years of this century, complementing his friend LeConte, who was unquestionably the range's most prominent explorer, mapmaker, and photographer. With his brother Edward and two other men, Hutchinson entered the mountains in mid-July with a bold goal: the ascent of the still unclimbed Mount Humphreys.

At Blaney Meadows the group encountered Gilbert and LeConte, the latter welcoming his Bay Area friends and begging to hear the news from home. "All the afternoon," LeConte wrote in his diary, "I talked with my friends, and smoked their cigars and drank their benedictine." The two parties traveled together as far as Colby Meadow, that exquisite spot at the head of Evolution Valley. (Readers familiar with Sierra geography may wonder why Hutchinson ignored Piute Creek, a far more direct route to Mount Humphreys.

Lacking lightweight food and equipment, early travelers depended greatly on pack animals to transport their necessities; Piute Creek, extremely rugged in its lower reaches, was not feasible for stock.)

Leaving LeConte and Gilbert to their explorations of the Goddard Divide, Hutchinson's group ascended a faint sheep path leading up the north wall of Evolution Valley. Soon they arrived at a superb campsite, a lake "fringed with the exquisite alpine heather," as Hutchinson later wrote. In the background loomed a multitude of unclimbed peaks; closer at hand the men were amused by the antics of dozens of gray-crowned rosy finches, those hyperactive denizens of the subalpine zone. The beautiful lake, situated on a high bench overlooking Evolution Valley, was named Lake Frances, after one man's wife. It was to lose this name in later years, appearing on the map simply as Lake 11,106.

A reconnaissance by two of the men to the top of nearby Glacier Divide—which they would have to cross to reach Mount Humphreys—provided a dramatic view of their goal, only four miles to the north. But the foreground terrain worried the men, for steep cliffs and ominous couloirs on the north side of the ridge looked difficult for humans and certainly impassable for stock. On the following day, having tethered their mules to shrubs along the shoreline of Lake Frances, the men were able, with only a few moments of apprehension, to cross the divide at what immediately was dubbed Snow-Tongue Pass. Four tired mountaineers set up camp that night in desolate Humphreys Basin.

At dawn on July 18 the quartet set off toward one of the range's most spectacular summits. Wary of facing the difficulties of the route attempted by LeConte and Cory, Hutchinson led his team up a different side of the mountain. Sheer cliffs blocked the upper part of this route also, but the confident Hutchinson made a courageous—or perhaps foolhardy—effort and succeeded in surmounting a frightfully exposed wall. Edward Hutchinson managed to struggle up a rope cast down by his brother, but their two companions demurred, contenting themselves with the ascent of a nearby pile of rocks they facetiously named Married Men's Point. A few minutes later, at precisely the moment LeConte strode alone onto the barren saddle of Muir Pass, the Hutchinson brothers clambered onto the exposed summit rocks of 13,986-foot Mount Humphreys. Another Sierra giant had fallen.

SIERRA CLUB OUTINGS

LeConte and Hutchinson were hardly the only wanderers in the High Sierra during the early years of the twentieth century. Although these two men were certainly the most ambitious and skillful mountaineers of this era, many fishermen and hikers also tramped through the mountains, investigating remote cirques and following streams to their sources. These pioneers occasionally published accounts of their journeys in such popular magazines as *Sunset* and *Overland Monthly.* During this same period, participants in the soon-to-be-famous Sierra Club outings began to publish articles in the *Sierra Club Bulletin,* thus conveying a vast body of information to other Club members and the general public. The inspiration for the first of these outings came to Will Colby in 1900. Upon learning of an Oregon club's recent summer trips to the Cascade Range, the twenty-five-year-old mining engineer approached the directors of the Sierra Club with a proposal for a Club-sponsored trip to Yosemite National Park. With the enthusiastic support of the organization's president, John Muir, Colby had little trouble convincing the hierarchy that his plan was feasible. Thus, in mid-July 1901, ninety-six Club members gathered in Yosemite Valley, the staging area for the journey toward their main camp at Tuolumne Meadows. Included in this group were Muir, his daughters Wanda and Helen, the noted landscape artist William Keith, and the chief of the United States Biological Survey, C. Hart Merriam. (Each of these five pioneers has since been honored by at least one Sierra place name.) Excited to be embarking on an adventure into the unknown, the trip participants nonetheless were saddened to learn that one of their most venerated members would not make the journey: renowned geologist Joseph LeConte, father of Joseph Nisbet LeConte, had died in Yosemite Valley a week earlier. The trip went on, of course, and Colby deemed it so spectacularly successful that he immediately drew up plans for a second excursion the following summer.

During the succeeding years, Club members, limited to about 200 per trip, repeatedly visited the most accessible areas of the Sierra: Yosemite, Kings Canyon, and the Mount Whitney region. On a trip to the latter in 1903, 103 outing members reached the highest point in the United States on the same day, a feat that William Frederic Badè, the chronicler of that year's outing, thought was "one of the most remarkable achievements in the history of mountaineering." Clarence King surely would have agreed.

The 1907 outing was a typical one. As usual, there had been a tremendous amount of behind-the-scenes planning during the preceding months. The exact itinerary had to be charted; packers and cooks had to be hired well in advance; and, at the last minute, the foodstuffs had to be purchased and packed. Will Colby handled most of this work himself, as he had done since 1901 and would do until 1930.

The locale chosen for the main base camp of 1907 was that marvelous blend of forest, rock, meadow, and water: Soda Springs, in Tuolumne Meadows. This was not unknown territory; Club members had been charmed by its pristine beauty in 1901 and again in 1904. The group spent a week at the idyllic site, then began working south across the Cathedral Range toward the headwaters country of the Merced River, territory previously unvisited by the Club. Strings of pack animals transported the paraphernalia necessary for the self-contained expedition. Huge iron stoves, cooking pots, bedding, and vast amounts of foodstuffs—all had to be balanced carefully onto the mules' backs. Packers, cooks, and their assistants broke camp as soon as possible after breakfast and traveled at a steady, rapid rate in order to have the next camp established by the time the outing participants arrived singly or in small groups.

Following dinner each night, the group would gather around a gigantic campfire to enjoy a program that might include lectures by eminent men of science, yarns spun by Civil War veterans, and performances by talented musicians. Group singing and hot drinks capped the evening's entertainment. Then, if one were fortunate, the almost unnaturally brilliant glow from the rising full moon would light the way to a soft bed beneath the lodgepole pines, the swift stream nearby providing that sublime neutral murmur that not only dampens the footfalls of unseen nocturnal creatures but also lulls one to sleep even before the myriad events of the day can be absorbed.

While most of the 1907 outing members fished and enjoyed short hikes in proximity to the camp at Washburn Lake, fifteen intrepid climbers loaded five days' worth of food onto their backs and headed east over virtually uncharted country toward distant Mount Ritter. Their pioneering route, now a segment of the High Route, crossed Blue Lake Pass, descended remote Bench Canyon to the North Fork of the San Joaquin River, and surmounted the steep but lovely shelves and slabs rising toward Mount Ritter. The previous winter's snowfall had been the heaviest since the harsh winter of 1894-95, and the trekkers found much of their route buried by snow. Nevertheless, in short order, all fifteen climbers stood atop the famous peak first climbed by their club's president thirty-five years earlier. Some days later, after all the outing members were reunited, Colby led them down the wild gorge of the Tuolumne River to civilization. The month-long outing of 1907 was over.

One of the participants in the knapsack trip to Mount Ritter was Marion Randall Parsons, a strong-willed woman who later wrote numerous eloquent articles for the *Sierra Club Bulletin*. Parsons especially craved Mount Ritter's summit on this trip, for she well remembered an event that had taken place three years earlier, when, as she wrote in 1908, her "feminine aspirations toward that very mountain were crushed by the stern masculine decree that fair ladies' backs were not fitted to bear such burdens." Needless to say, Parsons had no trouble with the routine ascent; indeed, she reveled in the "mysterious atmosphere" of the heights.

Women were welcomed on the Sierra Club outings, even if they often were discouraged from participating in strenuous activities. Females had been infrequent visitors to the timberline country in the nineteenth century, for there was widespread speculation that they couldn't withstand the rigorous life. Theodore Solomons had visited Tuolumne Meadows with four college women in 1896, finding them "considerably slower than athletic young men, but fully as able otherwise to cope with all the physical difficulties." For its day, this was a remarkably liberated belief, and not all of the male authors who later wrote for the *Bulletin* subscribed to this view of women's qualifications. Mount Humphreys, according to one writer, was "too dangerous to be undertaken by the ladies." Another climber wrote that before embarking on a side trip to a rugged area, "it was heartily agreed (by the boys) that the girls should be left behind to rest."

The many women who wrote for the *Bulletin* generally accepted their second-class roles with good humor. Elizabeth Cowles once wrote a five-page treatise entitled, "Have You a Mountain Widow in Your Home?" This article, directed toward male mountaineers, counsels them to introduce women to the timberline country slowly, with the eventual goal of sharing the mountain experience. Even though the gist of Cowles' article is admirable for its time, hikers of the 1990s may be amused by some of the advice: "Praise her endlessly." "Tell her how purty she looks." "Read aloud." And, if it rains for a solid

week, "take your girl friend back to the valley where she can get a
hot bath and go to the movies."

Females were not the only ones subjected to discrimination during the early years of Sierra exploration. Even the sainted Will Colby
was not free from prejudice, as evidenced by some of his recollections
published in the 1931 *Bulletin*. Charlie Tuck was a Chinese who served
as an extremely able and popular cook for the first thirteen outings.
"Poor Charlie" found himself lost on several occasions, episodes that
Colby attributed to the demon rum: "I can testify that Chinese gin
must be a very potent intoxicant." When Tuck died, "he left, for all
his Mongolian ancestry, many devoted admirers." For the 1920 outing the Sierra Club had hired as chief cook a Southern black named
Colonel Jones: "He brought with him as his help three other darkies,
who were as incompetent and lazy as he was capable and industri-
ous." Capable, that is, except for his biscuits, which "might have
served better in the bombardment of enemy trenches." In all his vo-
luminous writings, Colby never once castigated his fellow Caucasians
in this sarcastic manner; that wouldn't have been gentlemanly.

Participants in these early outings discovered that the weeks passed
pleasantly and far too quickly. Forgotten were concerns about work,
personal problems, and the unpleasant events already marring the new
century, such as a presidential assassination, rampaging anarchists in
Europe, brushfire wars in the Philippines and Nicaragua, and the
dreadful 1906 earthquake and fire in San Francisco (only eighty Club
members managed to find time for that summer's trip). The High Sierra became more clearly understood as a result of these early outings,
though much of the exploration was concentrated around the Sierra
Club's favorite locales: Yosemite and Kings Canyon.

END OF AN ERA

The central part of the Sierra became better known to the public after the United States Geological Survey's George Davis spent the
summer of 1907 charting the rugged country south of the Goddard
Divide. He became the first person to cross Muir Pass with pack animals, a feat LeConte—perhaps somewhat enviously—attributed to
the unusually heavy snowpack, which he thought would afford far
better footing for mules than the rough talus he had looked down
upon in 1904. Davis had gone on to descend the Middle Fork of the
Kings River, later crossing Cartridge Pass and exploring the Mount

Pinchot region. Davis's work of this summer emerged five years later with the publication of the "Mt. Goddard Quadrangle," a map regarded by many as a masterpiece of mountain cartography.

In the summer of 1908 LeConte, Hutchinson, and a Berkeley realtor named Duncan McDuffie set forth from Tuolumne Meadows with three mules and food for a month. Many segments of the high mountain route first envisioned by Theodore Solomons had been explored already, but the three men were well aware that no one had yet connected all of them. This was the trio's chief objective, but, as usual, other goals beckoned as well. For instance, halfway down the range rose the soaring crests of the Mount Abbot group; of its seven peaks, all rising above 13,000 feet, none had ever been attempted. Farther south, another feature intrigued LeConte. Six years earlier, from Split Mountain, he had spied a broad gap at the head of the South Fork of the Kings River. If pack animals could be led across this barrier—now known as Mather Pass—it would shorten the route by keeping it close to the main crest; the alternate route over Cartridge Pass lay several miles to the west.

For the first sixty miles of their journey, the three men followed the familiar ground along the Middle and South Forks of the San Joaquin River. Then, at Mono Creek, they turned east and headed upstream toward the northern outriders of the Mount Abbot group. From the summit of impressive Mount Mills, which they ascended from the head of the Fourth Recess, the men were stymied by the knife-edged ridge leading across to Mount Abbot, the area's prize summit. Unwilling to abandon their goal without examining the other aspects of the peak, the trio spent several days circling the Mono Divide on the west, returning to the subalpine region by means of the Hilgard Branch of Bear Creek. Their mountain proved more accessible from Lake Italy, and late in the afternoon of July 13 the men stood atop its 13,715-foot summit. There was no sign of previous ascent; indeed, LeConte felt "certain that no mountaineer had ever before been nearer than the peak of Seven Gables, six miles to the southwest." (Unaccountably, LeConte seems to have forgotten not only his own recent ascent of nearby Mount Mills, but the ascent, by both Brewer and Solomons, of Peak 12,691, two miles to the northwest.)

Returning from Mount Abbot's summit, LeConte and Hutchinson detoured to a broad saddle west of the peak. LeConte, realizing that the Second Recess probably could be reached from this pass, thought it would "make a great cut-off in the High Mountain Route." The planners of the John Muir Trail apparently regarded this gap—known today as Gabbot Pass—as impractical, with the result that it is now a wild and integral part of the High Route.

The three men continued their journey south and on July 18 successfully crossed Muir Pass, where the terrain proved even rougher than LeConte had anticipated. The three mules, the sturdiest money could buy, suffered badly, and by the end of the day their legs were caked with blood. But the terrain below became easier and easier, and in short order the expedition entered a great canyon that apparently overwhelmed LeConte. His article in the *Sierra Club Bulletin* is laced with praise; by turns, the canyon of the Middle Fork was "imposing," "glorious," and "beautiful." It seems altogether proper that this wild and serene place should bear the name of the person who described it so enthusiastically.

Leaving LeConte Canyon a short distance downstream, the party turned up Palisade Creek. A reconnaissance to Mather Pass was successful, but the men realized that their mules—sure-footed though they had proved on Muir Pass—could never surmount a series of steep cliffs and gullies just below the Palisade Lakes. Disappointed by this, the group instead worked up Cataract Creek toward Cartridge Pass. The remainder of the trip followed familiar and relatively easy terrain. After crossing Pinchot and Glen Passes, the trio descended to Vidette Meadow and followed Bubbs Creek to Kings Canyon. LeConte estimated they had traveled about 230 miles on the twenty-seven-day journey.

This expedition of 1908 can be said to have marked the completion of significant High Sierra exploration. The route followed by the three adventurers admirably fulfilled two of the three requirements set forth years earlier by Theodore Solomons. The "high mountain route" indeed paralleled the main crest, and it had been shown that if one used care, pack animals could be cajoled along it. But in numerous places it most definitely did not meet the third requirement: it could not be called a trail.

Realizing that not many people would attempt the arduous journey until a proper trail was established—and perhaps thinking of the vast new territory that could become accessible to their annual outings—the directors of the Sierra Club suggested to the California State Legislature that it would be in the public interest to construct and maintain a trail running the length of the Sierra. In 1915 the legislature appropriated $10,000, and work soon began on the trail, named in honor of the late president of the Sierra Club, John Muir. Several years later crews of young men had constructed a well-engineered path stretching between Yosemite and the southern ramparts of the range. Appropriations ran out before the trail could be built over two major obstacles—Mather and Forester Passes. But alternate routes sufficed, and Solomons' vision of a high mountain route was, by the mid-1920s, exemplified by the 210-mile-long John Muir Trail. Francis Farquhar spoke for many outdoors enthusiasts when he wrote that the new path was "a magnificent memorial, a highway for devout pilgrims blessing the memory of the prophet who was the first to sing the praises of this glorious sequence of mountain, meadow, pass, and lake."

Another symbol of the passing of the pioneering era concerns the formal diminishing of the range's *terra incognita*. In 1912 the United States Geological Survey published the last chart of its long-awaited set of High Sierra maps. With a scale of two miles to the inch, these well-executed quadrangles enabled prospective travelers to wander through the mountains with confidence. Understandably, these new maps contained errors: names sometimes were affixed to mountains other than the ones intended, and streams occasionally drifted into the wrong watersheds. But the blank sections that had characterized all previous maps finally had been filled in; no longer would hikers be obligated to climb a ridge to know what lay on the opposite side.

The appearance of these new maps, combined with the increasing ease by which the Sierra could be reached from the big cities, meant that vacationers soon thronged into the mountains, leading their pack animals along the newly charted paths. In spite of this influx, many remote sections of the timberline country remained infrequently visited during the next twenty years, for, as is true nowadays, hikers tended to congregate around beautiful locales easy of access.

Nevertheless, by the end of the 1930s, nearly every remote cirque and peak of the High Sierra had been visited, for during the period between the two world wars the last bastions of the unknown—the summits themselves—were conquered. Numerous mountain climbers of this period sought out the fine, untouched summits that had been ignored by the turn-of-the-century pioneers, but no one individual left his footprints upon so many of them as Norman Clyde. This scholar of the classics, who gave up a teaching career to spend more time in the mountains, began his Sierra climbing career in 1914, when he was in his late twenties. A half-century later he was the veteran of perhaps 1,000 ascents, of which 125 were either first ascents or new routes up previously ascended mountains.

During the 1920s and 1930s, the period of his most prolific climbing, Clyde served as a guide on numerous annual outings of the Sierra Club, thus becoming a well-known figure to many high-country travelers. An unhurried eccentric who transported a ninety-pound pack from one campsite to another, Clyde was also the detective who unerringly led searchers to the corpses of those who had come to grief on the crags. The man who sat, motionless, for hours against a lodgepole pine while absorbing *The Odyssey* in the original was also the consummate mountaineer who, without benefit of companionship, nonchalantly negotiated the vertical terrain of those very spires from which the overconfident had plummeted.

Compelling though the adventures of Norman Clyde are, one also must credit others who followed. In the 1930s a small cadre of Sierra Club rock climbers used ropes and pitons to reach dozens of minor, but spectacular, summits scattered throughout the range. Years later, a generation of technical rock climbers who had learned their craft on the huge walls of nearby Yosemite Valley arrived in the high country, establishing numerous multiday routes. The High Sierra—even its vertical planes of granite—was no longer a place of mystery.

Yet, from a High Route campsite at nightfall on a summer's day, the traveler of today gazes across a landscape little changed from that seen by the likes of Brewer, King, Solomons, and LeConte. As the remaining wisps of cumulus clouds dissolve in the alpenglow, the traveler might contemplate the following: the whisper of the brook in the distance soothed the pioneers also; the enormity of the full moon peering over the serrate crest astonished them also; the sudden cessation of the afternoon's breeze calmed them also. And, during this reverie, the traveler might—for a few moments—be transported gently back in time to stand side by side with the pioneers, wondering with them what new wonders tomorrow will bring.

Chapter Two

CIRQUE COUNTRY
KINGS CANYON TO DUSY BASIN

About five o'clock I camped for the night upon a charming knoll of shining granite, glacier-polished,—just across the stream from which grew plenty of feed [for Jack, the mule]. The timber line was near, and sweeping snow-fields patched the rocky walls of the mountains about and even below my little encampment. From some scrubby mountain pines near by I got bristly boughs—which Jack dragged to where I wanted them—and I built a good bed, resting, like an eagle's nest, upon the bare polished granite. Next came the cheery fire; and then, after a bath in the icy stream, I was prepared to enjoy the situation to the full, basking in the sun and studying the view down the cañon; for, softened as it was into a sort of mountain dreamland—a vision of the Delectable Mountains—in the warm haze of the afternoon sunshine, it was as grand and as beautiful a scene as ever my eyes beheld.

—Bolton Coit Brown,
from the May 1896 issue of the *Sierra Club Bulletin*

Kings Canyon is a marvelous place to begin an adventure into the timberline country of the High Sierra. This deep gorge, dominated by enormous ramparts of granite, has long been regarded as one of the premier sights of the range. Indians traveled through the canyon on their frequent trading journeys between the great central valley and Owens Valley, and there can be little doubt that they paused often in the sublime canyon to hunt game. Even today bear and deer roam the lush floor of the valley, and trout flash up and down the South Fork of the Kings River. Travelers who walk only a short distance from the highway will find themselves in a place little altered from the sanctuary the Indians once revered.

It is somewhat of a miracle that present-day visitors are able to enjoy the canyon in such a relatively pristine state, for after a road was built to Cedar Grove, around 1910, the canyon attracted numerous sightseers, some of whom harbored inappropriate thoughts. "Attempts have been made by certain irrigationists," wrote William Colby in 1926, "to secure permits to flood the Kings River Cañon. . . . It should be borne in mind that if these water-permits are once granted this region will be irrevocably mutilated and its value for national recreational purposes materially diminished for all time." The Sierra Club, ably represented by such farseeing men as Colby, Ansel Adams, Francis Farquhar, and Joel Hildebrand, campaigned for many years to save the canyon from exploitation, and finally, in 1940, Congress established Kings Canyon National Park. Yet even as late as 1952, the city of Los Angeles, that voracious user of water, had on file an application to construct a 155-foot-high dam on the Kings River immediately west of Cedar Grove, the village at the park boundary. This dam, and two additional dams planned for upstream, not only would have drowned Kings Canyon, but would have created a series of reservoirs extending into the very heart of the High Sierra. The project needed the upstream dam sites to be workable, and, fortunately, these were located inside the park. The water-power brokers turned their attention to other rivers.

Thus, instead of watching water-skiers at play upon a placid reservoir, the High Route traveler leaving road's end is able to appreciate a more pleasant vista: the glistening Kings winding silently through Zumwalt Meadows.

The hiker's initial objective is to surmount the Monarch Divide, the watershed boundary between the South and Middle Forks of the Kings River. Once this lofty ridge is attained, the High Route closely parallels it eastward as it becomes known as Cirque Crest. The word *cirque* in this place name proves accurate, for the traveler constantly walks up or across these common Sierra features. In essence, a cirque is a huge scoop in the flank of a mountain ridge. Ridges, or spurs, enclose the cirque on two sides; only the downhill side is open. This gap, of course, marks the exit path of the glacier responsible for carving the feature. The observant hiker can spot telltale traces of the former glacier in the form of highly polished granite slabs. More often than not, a lake or two reposes in the bottom of a cirque, adding to the charm of these geological wonders.

Cirque Crest and its extensions continue east to meet the main Sierra crest near Mather Pass. The High Route weaves through cirques and basins, crosses rugged ridges, and finally meets the Muir Trail just south of the pass. After following this famous path north for half a dozen miles, the High Route once again strikes out cross-country, traversing three passes before reaching Dusy Basin, the northern terminus of this segment of the route.

During the entire journey the hiker travels in the watershed of the Kings River. This turbulent stream, with its three major forks, dominates the geography of the south-central Sierra. The High Route trekker will not encounter the North Fork, for it lies far to the west of the main crest. He or she will, however, step across the other two rivers at their respective sources, a privilege reserved only for those who have walked many miles through a fabulous mountain wilderness.

APPROACHES

Kings Canyon, the southern terminus of the High Route, can be reached easily by following California State Highway 180 eastward from Fresno. The canyon's main administrative area, Cedar Grove, is reached about seven miles before the highway ends. Advice can be obtained at the Cedar Grove ranger station; a small store and several campgrounds are located nearby. The initial few miles of the High Route follow the Copper Creek Trail, which begins from the upper parking lot at road's end.

Hikers wishing to join the High Route from U.S. Highway 395, east of the Sierra crest, should use the Taboose Pass Trail; the approach road for this rugged path leaves the highway between the towns of Big Pine and Independence. After ten miles the trail ends at the Muir Trail; head north on this and join the High Route in Upper Basin.

Dusy Basin, the northern terminus of this segment of the High Route, can be reached in short order via the Bishop Pass Trail. See the "Approaches" section of Chapter 3 for details of this approach.

Loop trips can alleviate transportation problems considerably. Two of the most obvious trips can be made as follows. Hike the High Route until it intersects the Muir Trail in Upper Basin, then head south

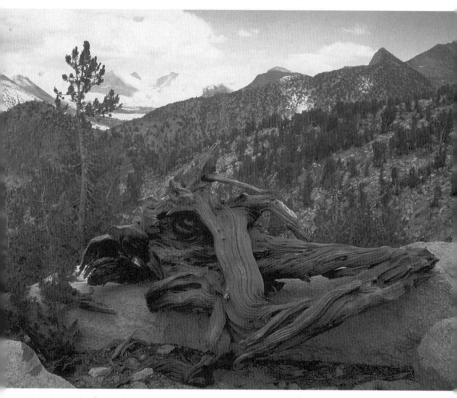

Weathered dead pine at timberline

on this famed path until reaching either the Woods Creek Trail or the Bubbs Creek Trail—both eventually lead down into Kings Canyon. The second loop follows the High Route all the way to Dusy Basin, then drops into LeConte Canyon. Follow the Middle Fork of the Kings River thirteen miles downstream to Simpson Meadow, where a trail surmounts the Monarch Divide and drops into Kings Canyon.

THE HIGH ROUTE
Kings Canyon to Grouse Lake
It is hardly surprising that the initial stage of most mountain journeys involves laborious uphill hiking. Coming at a time when the typical hiker is out of shape, unacclimated, and transporting the heaviest load of the entire trip, the seemingly endless hillsides can elicit rumblings from even the hardiest backpackers. The first section of the High

Route qualifies as a splendid example of such unremitting travel, for the hiker must toil up 6,000 feet to the first major pass, a disheartening prospect.

Optimistic hikers who seek the brighter side of unpleasant situations, however, will quickly discover mitigating factors on this interminable slope. The well-manicured trail zigzags up the north wall of Kings Canyon with such a gentle gradient that the traveler can slip into a rhythmic pace where the miles pass far more quickly than would be possible on a steeper, rockier path. Thus freed from scrutinizing the terrain immediately ahead, the hiker can better appreciate the two striking formations on the opposite side of the canyon. Directly across the way towers the enormous façade of Grand Sentinel, rising 3,500 feet above the meadows lining the valley floor. Several miles to the east lies the sculpted oddity known as the Sphinx, a delicate pinnacle capping a sweeping apron of granite. These two landmarks, visible for much of the ascent to the Monarch Divide, offer travelers a convenient means of gauging their progress; for instance, when one is finally level with the top of the Sphinx, the upward journey is two-thirds complete.

Hikers able to identify common Sierra trees have yet another method of measuring their progress, for the Copper Creek Trail, beginning at 5,050 feet from the end of the Kings Canyon Highway, ascends through numerous life zones, each of which is distinguished by a dominant conifer. On no other section of the High Route is the backpacker able to observe, during the space of a single day, such a variety of cone-bearing trees. One of these, the pinyon pine, will not be seen again during the remainder of the High Route, for it is absent from the western slope of the range north of this region. The observant hiker can spot several of these pines alongside the trail not far above road's end. Much more prominent during the early stages of the trek are the ponderosa pines, which rise amid vast thickets of manzanita and black oaks. These enormous evergreens, common on the western slope below 7,000 feet, are also unusual along the route, for they are replaced at higher elevations by the similar Jeffrey pine. Two other conifers—sugar pines and white firs—also are rarely seen along the High Route; they, too, prefer lower elevations. Specimens of these two trees can be found along the first few miles of the trail.

At 7,800 feet the path crosses a year-round stream at a place indicated on the topo map as Lower Tent Meadow. Hikers anticipating a brief respite from their tedious uphill journey will be sorely disappointed upon arrival here, for they will discover not a trace of a flat, grassy patch. As if to compound the euphemism, Upper Tent Meadow, a mile farther along, is even less of a meadow; it contains numerous willows and aspens bordering a creek that rushes down a fifteen-degree incline. Only a pilot flying overhead would call this light green swath of vegetation a meadow. (Bears frequent this area; campers beware!)

Regardless of the inappropriate nomenclature, both "meadows" offer travelers an excellent opportunity to shed their packs and examine the nearby conifers. Red firs make their first High Route appearance near the lower site; at the upper one, they are by far the dominant tree. The fir's scientific name, *Abies magnifica,* seems particularly suited for this stately giant, and the traveler well might agree with John Muir's assessment: "Even in the Sierra, where so many noble evergreens challenge admiration, we linger among these colossal firs with fresh love, and extol their beauty again and again, as if no other in the world could henceforth claim our regard."

Shortly beyond Upper Tent Meadow, a marvelous view opens up to the east. Three striking horns of granite pierce the sky eight miles distant. The sharp pyramid on the left is Mount Clarence King, one of the range's most difficult summits. The less spectacular peak to its right is Mount Cotter; farther right yet lies Mount Gardiner, displaying a tremendous western escarpment. All three of these jutting formations were named in honor of members of the California Geological Survey, which in 1864 explored the Kings Canyon region. Farther south, across the great canyon of the South Fork, are the massive peaks that make up the northern section of the Great Western Divide, the most significant subrange in the Sierra. It was from one of these peaks, Mount Brewer, that two members of the Survey spotted a lofty summit that they knew instantly must be the highest point in the state. They christened it Mount Whitney, in honor of the titular leader of the Survey.

Above the 9,500-foot mark the enormous red firs give way gradually to two new High Route evergreens, the western white pine and the lodgepole pine. The trunk of this latter conifer is smooth and ramrod-straight in this vicinity, as befits its common name; only at higher elevations, where it is more exposed to the wind, does the tree live up to its scientific name, *Pinus contorta.* The tree can be recognized by its distinctive needles, which grow in pairs and are extremely sharp.

At the 10,325-foot level, amid an extensive stand of lodgepole pines, the trail finally levels off and approaches a broad saddle offering a view westward toward Comb Spur. This welcome resting spot marks the beginning of a truly adventurous portion of the High Route, for here the hiker leaves the trail to begin wandering cross-country through the subalpine landscape. For the next thirty-five miles— mostly trailless—the High Route traveler almost always remains above the 10,000-foot level.

Leave the Copper Creek Trail near the saddle, contour due north through the open lodgepole forest for half a mile (staying in the trees, not the fragile meadows below) until reaching the creek dropping from Grouse Lake. Now ascend gentle terrain to the lakeshore. This pleasant body of water occupies the floor of a lovely cirque, the first of many such glacial basins to be encountered by the High Route traveler. Hikers wishing to add yet another conifer to their ever-growing list can easily spot the whitebark pine, the five-needled conifer that shares the shoreline with the lodgepole. These two evergreens are by far the most common trees along the High Route; not a single day passes without one or the other's presence.

Grouse Lake to Goat Crest Saddle

Work around either shore of Grouse Lake, then begin ascending north toward Grouse Lake Pass, the obvious low saddle northeast of Peak 11,354 (11,320+ on The Sphinx quad). Shortly after leaving the lake, the traveler encounters typical High Route terrain for the first time. Grassy benches and ramps, surrounded on all sides by shimmering granite, offer remarkably easy upward progress. Wildflowers and dwarf willows cover the landscape. Ancient snags, carved and etched by howling winter winds, pierce the unbelievably blue sky. Coming so soon after the monotonous, forested trail, this classic example of timberline country seems especially wondrous.

From 11,050-foot Grouse Lake Pass there is a superb view. To the south, beyond the Mount Brewer group, rise the distinct shapes of the Kaweah Peaks Ridge, that isolated group of summits that so dominate the southern Sierra. Close at hand to the east is the uninspiring mass of Goat Mountain, the highest summit of the region. Less than two miles to the west reposes marvelous Granite

Grouse Lake, with the Great Western Divide in the distance

Lake, a pleasantly shaped body of water encircled by acres of gleaming granite slabs.

One might be tempted to work left toward Granite Lake—but don't. The next High Route pass is now visible, a mere mile and a half to the north. To the right of a cluster of three small, rocky peaks lies the U-shaped saddle known as Goat Crest Saddle. Contour northeast from Grouse Lake Pass for several hundred feet, then angle down a gentle, grassy ramp toward the meadow-covered valley below. At about 10,900 feet, amid a profusion of shooting stars and other flowers, cross a meandering brook. Continue north over rolling meadowlands, past Lake 10,979, to Goat Crest Saddle, which lies midway between Peaks 11,797 and 12,059 (11,822 and 12,000+ on the new Marion Peak quad). This amazingly gentle pass, near the three-way junction of the Monarch Divide, Goat Crest, and Cirque Crest, marks the watershed boundary separating two great Sierra rivers, the South and Middle Forks of the Kings River. For nearly all of its next forty-odd miles—until Muir Pass—the High Route remains in this latter watershed. As if to inform the hiker of this fact, the pass offers a magnificent view of the symbols of the Middle Fork region, the Palisade group. Etched against the skyline, exactly fifteen miles distant, this cluster of jagged peaks includes four summits over 14,000 feet.

Goat Crest Saddle to Horseshoe Lakes

The north side of Goat Crest Saddle is by no means as gentle as the southern approach, and for the first time on the High Route the hiker encounters steep and rough terrain, along with year-round snowfields. Massive aprons of granite drop abruptly toward the highest of the four Glacier Lakes, and the traveler should keep to the left on the uppermost section to avoid the even steeper slabs directly below the pass. Only the top 150-foot section is at all tricky; a short scouting trip will reveal class 2-3 slabs separating the snowpatches. Once this section is overcome, the hiker can move with alacrity down the grassy ramps leading to the lakeshore.

Go around the lake on either side via easy walking along meadows and sandy beaches. From the lake's outlet there is a completely new view of the peaks to the north. The distinctive horn on the left side of this vista is remote Charybdis, the sinister spike guarding the entrance to one of the wildest canyons in the range, the Enchanted Gorge. To its right, a few miles closer, lies the most prominent visible peak, the black and forbidding mass of the high point of the Devil's Crags. Also visible is that section of the Sierra crest running from flattened Mount Powell southeast to triangular Mount Agassiz.

Drop down glacier-polished slabs to the next Glacier Lake, a pleasant pond surrounded by thirty-foot-high lodgepole pines. Not far below this lake, the hiker suddenly arrives at the brink of a 300-foot dropoff. Wooded ramps on the far left are easy; an alternate route proceeds down the eastern side of the creek. Following the stream is not recommended.

Whichever route is chosen, the hiker soon arrives at the extensive meadows forming the floor of Glacier Valley. Easy strolling through a dense forest of lodgepole pines leads, after one mile, to the State Lakes Trail, a distinct path intersected at 9,900 feet. Turn right onto this trail and follow it as it ascends a steep hillside to the lowest State Lake. The trail veers left midway along the northern shore of this lake and climbs north through the forest to the outlet of the next lake.

From this point, at 10,450 feet, the path becomes fainter and thus harder to follow. It contours three-quarters of a mile northwest, then surmounts a short but steep hillside—an ancient moraine. At its top, a sandy flat, one might see the unobtrusive sign indicating the trail to Horseshoe Lakes. Follow this trail north through the open forest.

Horseshoe Lakes to White Pass

The maintained trail fades out upon reaching the first Horseshoe Lake, and the High Route traveler next embarks on a mostly trailless section across an untrammeled landscape replete with history. For it was from this spot, in the summer of 1935, that members of the Sierra Club's annual outing set forth upon a journey that never has—and almost certainly never will be—repeated in the same manner. More than 100 hikers, accompanied by numerous pack animals, somehow managed to weave their way across the ridges and basins lying between Horseshoe Lakes and Lake Basin. Although this route had been scouted previously by outing managers, the three-day crossing involved laborious trailbuilding to ensure safe passage for the stock. Some traces of this manmade path exist today, and an occasional rusted horseshoe still may be seen. Present-day hikers able to envision a seemingly endless chain of humans and animals traversing this hostile terrain hardly can fail to appreciate the tenacity of these robust pioneers.

Work north from the first Horseshoe Lake for 300 yards until meeting the largest Horseshoe Lake. Proceed north along its western shore, then begin ascending the gentle, forested slope rising to the north. (Keep going in the same general direction all this time; don't head northeast up steeper terrain.)

Although the hiker might spy a ducked path in this forest, finding a trail is not necessary, for the traveling here is remarkably straightforward. Continue north for about half a mile (and perhaps 300 feet of elevation gain from the lake) until reaching an inconspicuous ridgecrest offering a view north toward the Devil's Crags. Turn right ninety degrees and hike eastward up this ridge, following a distinct path near the edge of the cliff that drops precipitously into Windy Canyon. The panorama increases with each step; soon, for the first time, the traveler is able to gaze straight down the great gash of the Middle Fork toward the naked hump of Tehipite Dome, one of the range's preeminent landmarks.

Continue upward along the path, closely following the curving rim overlooking Windy Canyon. Shortly after passing a tarn at 11,000 feet, the faint path subtly crosses Windy Ridge and commences an abrupt, 300-foot descent down a sandy incline to the lake shown on the topo map just east of the letter "n" in "Windy" (below the "W" in "WINDY" on the new Marion Peak quad).

From this beautiful pond, located at 10,700 feet, follow a wooded ledge eastward to Gray Pass, an inconspicuous saddle overlooking the valley of the South Fork of Cartridge Creek. Drop down, but not too abruptly, into a long, grassy gully that debouches into this infrequently visited valley, meeting the creek at approximately 10,200 feet.

Proceed upstream, passing soulful lakes and myriad granite boulders dappled with striking dark gray patches, inclusions known to geologists as xenoliths—"foreign rocks." Turn east almost anywhere and stroll upward into a wild cirque; then work up lush meadowlands and gentle ramps to the three adjacent tarns shown on the map. In this area the hiker wanders amid the loveliest possible terrain, where intimate streams meander through meadows dotted with granite blocks and wildflowers.

Deer are attracted to this idyllic spot also, and in September one might spy four-point bucks prowling the timberline country in search of does. On rare occasions these magnificent stags may be spotted far above timberline; perhaps they are traveling across ridges into adjoining basins.

Looking up the gentle slope to the northeast, the hiker can see the next High Route landmark, White Pass. This inconspicuous feature, lying low on the northwest ridge of Marion Peak, can be distinguished by the monolithic white slabs and blocks that comprise a relatively level saddle. Named in 1935 by the Sierra Club expedition, the 11,700-foot pass is an easy stroll from the west.

White Pass to Marion Lake

The opposite side of White Pass, however, is far more rugged. Straight across the rocky terrain to the northeast rises the obvious red cone called Red Point; to its right, at the viewer's level, lies Red Pass, the next objective. The terrain between the two passes proves far more complex than the previous section, as it involves loose blocks and circuitous class 2 slabs and gullies.

From White Pass scramble up the ridgecrest toward Marion Peak for about fifty vertical feet, then leave the ridge and begin contouring east across blocky granite. After proceeding in this manner for a few hundred yards, begin descending ramps and shallow gullies filled with debris. Continue downward until about fifty vertical feet below Red Pass; at this point the hiker can easily attain a loose but gentle slope that leads to the pass.

Upon reaching this well-named saddle (the granite has given way to rust-colored slate), the traveler can look down the opposite side and see, some 1,200 feet below, part of Marion Lake, the next High Route goal. Above and east of this sparkling body of water lies vast Lake Basin, speckled with ponds, lakes, and meadows. Beyond this basin rises the imposing ridge separating Lake Basin from Upper Basin; the High Route crosses this massive barrier at Frozen Lake Pass, the notch seen to the immediate right of the pyramidal peak near the ridge's left end. South of this notch, behind the low saddle just right of Vennacher Needle, towers the great bulk of Split Mountain, the southernmost 14,000-foot summit of the Palisade group.

From Red Pass descend an easy but tedious slope down toward Marion Lake. Snowfields linger until late season, affording excellent glissading opportunities when the snow is soft. Interspersed among the dwarf willows and grassy shelves are short sections of talus. However, there are no real obstacles in this area, and after a descent of nearly 1,000 feet the hiker reaches a meadow containing a tarn. Just below this welcome resting place is a short steep cliff that drops precipitously into Marion Lake. Here the hiker is confronted with a choice of several gullies. Although any one of these chutes may be followed, the easiest is the one on the left. How the 1935 Sierra Club group managed to cajole their mules down this obstacle remains a mystery. One trip participant later recalled this odious gash as a "steep chimney that, at first sight, looked impassable."

On a triangular boulder near the northern shore of Marion Lake is a plaque commemorating the person for whom the lake was named, Helen Marion Gompertz LeConte. Although Stanford professor Bolton Coit Brown was the first to describe this beautifully situated body of water, it is Joseph N. LeConte and his wife, Helen, who are more historically associated with the feature. Using the steep and arduous sheep track up Cartridge Creek as their approach route, the pair camped at Marion Lake several times during the early years of this century. It was from this base camp that LeConte made the first ascents of three of the eleven Sierra peaks that rise above the 14,000-foot mark: Split Mountain, Mount Sill, and North Palisade. Helen LeConte, who accompanied her husband on the 1902 adventure to Split Mountain, died in 1924; the plaque was affixed the following year.

Marion Lake to Frozen Lake Pass

From the outlet of Marion Lake follow a well-worn path that winds up a hillside to meet the inconspicuous track of the former Muir Trail. Not maintained since 1938, when the new trail was rerouted over Mather Pass, the old trail has all but vanished.

Continue up toward Lake Basin, passing a large, L-shaped lake, to an enormous meadow at 10,800 feet. Leave the traces of the old trail here and stroll north along the western edge of the meadow until clear of the swampy section. The next major feature of the High Route, Frozen Lake Pass, is not quite visible from this point, and route-finding problems are further complicated because the next section is represented on three different 15-minute quadrangles: Marion Peak, Mt. Pinchot, and Big Pine. (The same dilemma exists on the new 7.5-minute maps: you'll use Marion Peak, Mount Pinchot, and Split Mtn. Using one of the new composite maps solves this problem.) Using these maps in conjunction with a careful study of the terrain, the traveler can pick out the general location of Frozen Lake Pass: it is the first deep notch to the right of Peak 12,880+ (3,840+ meters on the Split Mtn. quad), a conspicuous pyramidal peak near the northern end of the ridge that borders the basin on the east. The correct pass also is identifiable as the second one north of Vennacher Needle, the imposing (but not needlelike) mass near the middle of the same ridge.

From the meadow proceed northeast up gentle timberline country, aiming for the lower right edge of the pyramidal peak. When abeam this feature, at about 11,600 feet, the hiker arrives at a large lake encircled by talus. (The Mt. Pinchot quadrangle depicts the southern one-third of this lake; the Big Pine quadrangle depicts the northern two-thirds.) Here, for the first time, the traveler obtains a close view of the southern side of Frozen Lake Pass, the left-hand notch of the two notches seen above the lake's end.

Frozen Lake Pass, one of the two or three most difficult sections of

Encroaching fog, Lake Basin

the High Route, has a fascinating history. In 1902 the two LeContes and Curtis Lindley knew they must cross the rugged barrier separating Lake Basin from Upper Basin if they were to reach their goal, Split Mountain. On July 23, Lindley, climbing solo, reached what is now Vennacher Col, the broad saddle just south of Vennacher Needle. Undoubtedly shaken after surmounting the exposed class 3 cliff leading to the col, Lindley must have given the opposite side only a cursory glance, for that night he informed the LeContes that "the eastern side of the divide was a precipice." (In reality, he had climbed the hardest section; the east side is class 2.)

On July 24 the threesome decided to explore the ridgecrest north of Vennacher Needle. Climbing a steep, loose talus slope to the right-hand notch visible from the lake at 11,600 feet, they found that the opposite side was truly a precipice, one far too dangerous to descend. Frustrated once again, the trio decided to traverse across the steep and unpleasant terrain to the next pass north. Here, to their "inexpressible joy," the pioneers looked down a steep but passable slope covered with talus and snowfields. The way to Upper Basin would not be easy, they knew, but at least no cliffs intervened. After their success on Split Mountain the following day, the LeContes and Lindley recrossed Frozen Lake Pass. But no one revisited the 12,350-foot notch until 1922, when Chester Versteeg named it after the perpetually ice-covered tarn immediately below the pass on the north. During the next six decades only seven more parties signed the historic register that reposes in a cairn astride the pass.

The obvious route from the lake at 11,600 feet to Frozen Lake Pass involves steep talus. Hikers should take their time, carefully testing—from the side—the stability of all boulders they plan to use. The vast majority of these boulders are solid—but all it takes is one rogue giant to crush a leg. *Be careful!* The party should also spread out horizontally so that any loosened blocks will crash harmlessly below.

Upon cresting the pass the traveler gazes straight across the barren, lake-dappled tundra of Upper Basin toward enormous Split Mountain, less than four miles distant. The view to the south is spectacular also, with dozens of peaks, mostly unnamed, piercing the skyline. Directly in line with Cartridge Pass, a well-known landmark on the former Muir Trail, rises Arrow Peak, easily recognized by its knife-edged ridges.

Frozen Lake Pass to Cirque Pass

The terrain on the north side of Frozen Lake Pass is far more rugged than that encountered on the south side. The initial class 2-3 slope, quite steep, contains extremely unstable rock, and it is difficult to avoid instigating small rockslides. Hikers should move one at a time during this nasty descent, once again making sure that no one lingers in the fall line below. (Steep snow on the right may offer better progress, but don't try this when the snow is hard or when the runout looks rocky.) Fortunately, this traumatic section is short, and the traveler soon reaches a permanent snowfield that provides safe glissading in the afternoon, when the snow is soft.

Shortly after passing the frozen tarn, the hiker arrives at yet another disheartening dropoff. Head left on a diagonal while descending this 300-foot talus slope, aiming for a round lake at 11,500 feet. This feature signifies the end of the difficult crossing; the traveler finally has reached the appealing landscape surrounding the headwaters of the South Fork of the Kings River.

Work east across the flower-covered tundra of Upper Basin, heading in the direction of Split Mountain. After one mile the hiker intersects the High Sierra's most famous manmade feature, the Muir Trail. Hikers who follow this well-worn path to the south will stand atop Mount Whitney in sixty miles; the trail's other terminus,

Yosemite Valley, lies 150 miles to the north. During their journey to Yosemite National Park, High Route trekkers will follow the Muir Trail for a total of about thirty miles, staying within a few air miles of it for much of the remaining distance.

Follow the trail north toward Mather Pass, the distinct saddle visible a mile away. Soon after striding up the superbly constructed switchbacks on the south side of the col, the backpacker stands astride the saddle, ready to re-explore the Middle Fork region. The views from the 12,100-foot pass are striking, especially to the north, where the dark spikes of the Palisade group dominate the panorama. Nestled in the fiordlike glacial canyon in the foreground are the two Palisade Lakes, bordered on the northeast by the serrated bulk of Middle Palisade.

Mather Pass first was visited in 1897, when a sheepman apparently negotiated the rough crossing with his burro. By the early 1920s it was certain that the Muir Trail would be rerouted over the lofty saddle, named in 1921 in honor of Stephen Mather, the first director of the National Park Service. For various reasons, it was not until 1938 that the last link of the famed trail was built, capping an effort that had begun nearly a quarter of a century earlier.

After dropping abruptly from the pass, the Muir Trail levels out as it approaches the Palisade Lakes. When opposite the upper lake, the hiker obtains a fine view of the next High Route landmark, Cirque Pass. This saddle can be spotted high above the grassy, slab-covered cliff rising above the far end of the lower lake.

Leave the trail about 100 yards beyond the outlet of the lower lake and begin moving diagonally upward to the west, aiming for the grassy cliff seen several hundred feet above. There are many ways to ascend this 300-foot-high barrier, most of which involve short stretches of class 2-3 scrambling. One of the easiest routes lies at the far left, where talus-covered shelves zigzag up the left edge of the cliff. Those who attempt the central portion of the cliff should expect to encounter exposed class 3 sections between wet, grassy slabs.

After topping this steep obstacle, the High Route hiker will have little trouble following the gently angled slabs and gullies that lead, after 1,000 feet, to the obvious, broad saddle northeast of Peak 12,220 (12,200+ on the North Palisade quad). Cirque Pass, at 12,100 feet, offers an excellent view south toward the jagged, unnamed peaks west of Mather Pass. To the north, mighty North Palisade dominates the horizon, its precipitous cliffs towering above the next High Route obstacle, Potluck Pass. In the foreground lies barren Lake 11,672 (3,559 meters on the Split Mtn. quad), an enormous body of water that occupies most of the floor of the classically shaped cirque west of Palisade Crest.

Cirque Pass to Knapsack Pass

From Cirque Pass drop down a few feet toward the lake, then begin working left down a series of interconnected shelves. By looking around carefully in this area, the hiker can avoid class 3 sections. Within several hundred feet the terrain eases, and the traveler soon stands at the pleasant outlet stream of Lake 11,672. It was along this beautiful watercourse—now known as Glacier Creek—that Joseph N. LeConte, James Hutchinson, and two companions tramped in 1903 during their quest for the highest summits of the Palisades.

Cross the outlet, stroll across lovely, glacier-polished slabs, then ascend a narrow, grassy slot on the minor knoll rising immediately to the north. Work northeast along the top of this hill until it is feasible to drop down toward the small lake nestling beneath Potluck Pass, the low, flat saddle northeast of Peak 12,692 (12,698 on the North Palisade quad).

From afar, the upper part of this pass looks impassable because of steep, monolithic cliffs. In reality, however, hidden-from-below ledges afford a surprisingly easy class 2 route. Ascend an inconspicuous path up a short, unpleasant scree slope lying left of the cliffs that drop from the pass. When the path fades, follow a series of narrow shelves that slant up and across to the saddle.

Due north, only one mile distant, looms the complex southwest wall of North Palisade. One can only wonder why the 1903 pioneers, upon reaching this vantage point, didn't abandon their effort, for no obvious route exists on the craggy, 1,500-foot face. Apparently undeterred by the sobering sight, the men worked their way over to the base of the wall, discovered a hidden chute, and managed eventually to stand atop the Sierra's third-highest summit.

Two miles west of Potluck Pass, across huge Palisade Basin, lies the next High Route saddle, Knapsack Pass. Five hundred feet lower than Potluck, it is the rounded saddle to the left of pyramidal Columbine Peak. A circuitous but easy section of the High Route now begins: the crossing of Palisade Basin and Knapsack Pass. Virtually no talus is encountered, and the gradient proves tame in comparison with the rugged segment just completed.

From Potluck Pass contour toward North Palisade, then curve left, aiming for an inconspicuous saddle a little lower than Potluck and half a mile distant. After reaching this flattened saddle begin a gradual but roundabout descent to the largest Barrett Lake, which is met at its southeast shore.

Following a path, circle this deep blue body of water on its east and north sides. Upon reaching the northwest side of the lake, climb a small bluff and descend gentle slabs west to the next lake, a fine place to pause and absorb the panorama. In the foreground to the south lies a strikingly beautiful lake that snakes through a small canyon. Farther south, across the enormous trench of Palisade Creek, rise the great peaks surrounding Amphitheater Lake. Dominating the view to the east is the fearsome wall stretching between Thunderbolt Peak and North Palisade.

Knapsack Pass, lying only 200 feet above the level of the lake, is now prominent to the west. Wander up and across slabs, talus, and gullies via any of numerous possible routes—all circuitous—to the saddle, at 11,673 feet. Looking west from this pleasant site, the hiker obtains a superlative view of one of the Sierra's most distinctive subranges, the Black Divide. Near the northern end of this nine-mile-long ridge rises the dark bulk of Black Giant, a peak soon to be seen at close range by the High Route traveler. Closer at hand, in line with this prominent peak, lies the glaciated gorge of LeConte Canyon, which curves westward toward Muir Pass, a lofty saddle hidden behind Black Giant.

Knapsack Pass to Dusy Basin

A straightforward class 2 route zigzags down the granite slabs below Knapsack Pass toward the chain of lovely lakes in lower Dusy Basin. As one approaches these shallow ponds, willows appear and can cause difficulties—stay away from the stream here. Soon, stands of conifers offer a welcome respite from the travails of the past few days. Without question, Dusy Basin is the most verdant High Route locale since Marion Lake.

Because of the basin's beauty, and because the nearest road is only eight miles away, the site has attracted hordes of backpackers and fishermen over the years; many of these wilderness lovers unwittingly

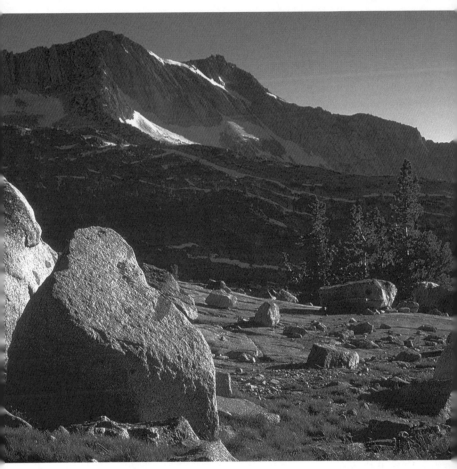

Late afternoon at Dusy Basin

have left traces of their visits. Blackened boulders are evidence of once-roaring campfires; trampled dusty areas, further marred by trenches, denote former tent platforms. This is one of the most abused areas in the range. Fortunately, wilderness authorities have reacted: those who travel with stock are not allowed to camp here. This restriction, coupled with backpackers' new awareness of the wilderness ethic, could mean that this beautiful region will suffer little further damage and may, in a century, recover.

This segment of the High Route ends at the first lake of the chain, a shallow pond surrounded by sedges, wildflowers, and granite slabs.

REVERSING THE ROUTE

The first problem encountered while traveling the High Route north to south occurs in Dusy Basin, where the traveler must locate Knapsack Pass. This is not too difficult if the hiker begins from the lowest lakes in the basin. Looking southeast from here, the viewer can easily spy a rounded saddle to the right of the bold pyramid of Columbine Peak. The route to the pass itself involves straightforward class 2 slabs and gullies.

From Knapsack Pass do not drop down too far before beginning to move diagonally left toward the next-to-largest Barrett Lake. After circling the basin's largest lake on its north and east shores, work eastward up complex terrain undistinguished by major landmarks. When directly beneath mighty North Palisade, however, the hiker is afforded a close view of Potluck Pass: it is the easy-to-reach saddle immediately left of ragged Peak 12,692.

The descent from Potluck Pass appears steep and difficult, and it can be if the easiest route is not found. From the pass, walk down a long, diagonal ramp leading southwest. When this fortuitous feature vanishes, scramble down a series of easy, interconnecting shelves leading in the same general direction. After a short distance the hiker attains a scree slope leading downward to much easier terrain.

From nearby Lake 11,672 the route to Cirque Pass is not at all obvious. From the outlet of the lake climb up and slightly right for about 100 vertical feet. At this point it is possible to follow a series of connected granite shelves that slice up and left to the low point northeast of Peak 12,220.

The final routefinding problem encountered before reaching the Muir Trail occurs above the lower Palisade Lake. There the hiker must descend a slabby, 300-foot-high cliff. The easiest route probably lies at the far right, where class 2-3 terrain leads down toward a small, white dome visible below.

Locating Frozen Lake Pass is easy if the traveler begins looking for it from the series of trailside tarns south of Mather Pass. As seen from here, the correct pass is the second deep notch to the right of the most prominent peak to the southwest, Vennacher Needle. Exactly where the hiker leaves the trail to head for this pass is immaterial, since the tundra of Upper Basin makes for generally easy walking. The ascent to the pass itself is fairly obvious from below.

Few routefinding problems are found on the next section to Marion

Lake, but here the High Route hiker faces a dilemma. Rising above the western shore of the lake are major talus chutes. The easiest route lies in the second-from-right gully, where a faint path may be followed. The other chutes are all passable, but they are longer, steeper, or looser.

The next problem makes itself known at Red Pass, for the terrain on the west side is complex and landmarks are few. Drop down about fifty feet from the pass, then begin gently ascending across class 2 gullies and shelves. When White Pass is first seen, immediately left of several prominent, light-colored outcrops, contour across toward it, making sure the ridge crest is reached above the pass, not below it. In this manner class 3-4 slabs can be avoided.

From the beautiful meadowlands below the west side of White Pass the hiker can pick out, across the gulf formed by the South Fork of Cartridge Creek, the next objective, Gray Pass. This minor feature can be recognized as the low, gray-colored saddle immediately to the left of two white peaklets.

After climbing a long gully to Gray Pass, contour west across a wooded bench to a lovely pond. Ascend the steep hillside beyond, cross Windy Ridge, and then curve down southwest along the top of the cliffs overlooking Windy Canyon. Soon it is possible to leave this curving ridge and wander down south through a dense forest to the Horseshoe Lakes.

Farther south, be careful not to miss the creek that flows down Glacier Valley from the Glacier Lakes. This stream crossing lies about a mile below the second of the States Lakes. At the head of Glacier Valley the imposing wall can be climbed easily on the far right, by means of wooded slabs.

From the upper Glacier Lake it is easy to recognize the next High Route landmark, Goat Crest Saddle: it is the deep, U-shaped pass to the southwest. The route to this col is rather obvious, even though the hiker must weave through massive slabs of granite and circumvent steep snowfields.

From this saddle, look carefully to find the next landmark, Grouse Lake Pass. Lower than the viewer's level, it lies immediately left of rocky Peak 11,354. Framed perfectly in the saddle is the distant pyramid of Mount Hutchings.

After reaching the long meadow below Grouse Lake, make sure to contour, not descend, to the southwest. Failing to do so will cause the hiker to miss the Copper Creek Trail, an embarrassing situation.

ALTERNATE ROUTES

Few alternate routes exist along this initial segment of the High Route, for vast gorges and rugged ridges dictate that the hiker generally negotiate the route as laid out. Still, several choices are available, and these are explained below.

Hikers wishing to bypass the lovely High Route country lying between Grouse Lake and Glacier Valley can do so by remaining on the Copper Creek Trail as it descends into exquisite Granite Basin. The trail continues north over Granite Pass, later curving east to join the High Route above Dougherty Meadow.

The mere thought of climbing over difficult Frozen Lake Pass into Upper Basin might discourage less experienced High Route trekkers. There are two alternatives to this traumatic pass: Vennacher Col and Cartridge Pass. Vennacher Col, located immediately south of Vennacher Needle, is neither as loose nor as strenuous as Frozen Lake Pass, but is technically more difficult; on the west side of the col is an exposed 100-foot cliff. Persons experienced in class 3 climbing will have no trouble with this obstacle. Upper Basin is reached in short order from the pass.

The second alternative, though far easier than either Frozen Lake Pass or Vennacher Col, requires a significant detour from the High Route. This tough variation, indicated on the old topo map as a trail, follows the traces of the former Muir Trail over Cartridge Pass, descends 2,000 feet to the South Fork of the Kings River, and continues up this stream into Upper Basin. The old trail over the pass and down to the river has mostly disappeared, and the hiker will encounter talus and other nasty sections.

MOUNTAINEERING

Goat Mountain

One of the great Sierra viewpoints is a peak with such a prosaic name that it often is overlooked by hikers. Goat Mountain, easily accessible from Grouse Lake via class 2 terrain, probably was climbed by James Gardiner and Charles Hoffmann during the survey of 1864; they reported reaching a lofty peak in this area. The isolated 12,207-foot mass soon attracted curious hikers. Helen Gompertz (who later married her old friend, Joseph N. LeConte), climbed it in 1896, remarking in a *Sierra Club Bulletin* article that "others have already called attention to the fine panoramic view of the whole Sierra uplift from this peak, and our subsequent trips to higher mountains in no wise interfered with the verdict that the Goat Mountain view is unsurpassed in its kind." Naturally, the "whole Sierra uplift" is not visible, but the entire fifty-mile section of the crest lying between the Whitney and Evolution groups stands out sharply against the eastern sky. To the south, across the 7,200-foot-deep trench of the South Fork of the Kings River, rise the lofty peaks of the Great Western Divide.

Windy Point

Another classic Sierra vantage point, reached by a mere half-hour level detour from the High Route, is Windy Point. Indicated on the 15-minute map simply as Peak 11,150 (11,200+ on the new Marion Peak quad), this bump at the northern end of Windy Ridge provides a stupendous view of the gorge of the Middle Fork of the Kings River, two miles distant and 5,000 feet below. Ansel Adams and Cedric Wright, two eminent photographers of the Range of Light, visited this viewpoint during the Sierra Club's outing of 1935; several of their magnificent photographs were published in the next year's annual *Sierra Club Bulletin.* To reach Windy Point, leave the High Route as it crosses Windy Ridge and walk out the spur to the "summit," a pleasing group of weathered granite boulders. The aesthetics of this outcrop are somewhat marred by the presence of an unmanned radio repeater.

At Windy Point, with the canyon of the Middle Fork of the Kings below

Marion Peak

Marion Peak, offering yet another sublime view, can be reached from the High Route by following the well-delineated class 3 ridge rising above White Pass. The highest point along Cirque Crest, it was climbed first in 1902 by Joseph N. LeConte and Curtis Lindley; the two pioneers ascended from Marion Lake to reconnoiter the surrounding countryside.

Peak 11,553

A minor summit commanding a striking view of Lake Basin and the great canyon of Cartridge Creek is Peak 11,553 (11,440+ on the new Marion Peak quad). This viewpoint, first reached by Bolton Coit Brown in 1895, can be climbed from Marion Lake in the following manner: walk around the east shore of the lake, ascend alongside the obvious creek nearly to the next higher lake, then wander up the class 2 slabs and talus above. The summit is reached in short order. The escarpment on the north side of the peak is most impressive.

Mount Ruskin

Mount Ruskin, the southernmost point of the jagged ridge separating Lake Basin from Upper Basin, is a stimulating class 3 scramble from Cartridge Pass. In a *Sierra Club Bulletin* article, Bolton Coit Brown described his 1895 ascent as "the most aerial and dangerous climbing that I ever happened to attempt." Regarding his handholds, the professor supposed that "an inch or two of solid rock is as safe as a yard or two—but somehow you don't feel the same about it." Present-day climbers still encounter Brown's "aerial" sections, but there are no real difficulties on the long, curving ridge.

Split Mountain

The easiest major peak in proximity to the High Route proves to be 14,058-foot Split Mountain. The standard route leaves the Muir Trail south of Mather Pass and proceeds past Lake 11,599 to the broad saddle separating Mount Prater from Split Mountain. Horses were taken to this point during a 1943 survey, which indicates the lack of difficulty thus far. Basketball-sized talus perched at a thirty-degree angle constitutes the remaining 1,500 feet to the summit. Although often rated class 1, this slope is definitely class 2. Still, hikers encounter few problems en route to the summit, where a magnificent panorama awaits. The town of Big Pine, a dozen miles to the northeast, lies more than 10,000 feet below, and the traveler is acutely conscious of standing atop one of the earth's greatest escarpments. Genny Schumacher, editor of *Deepest Valley*, a comprehensive guide to the Owens Valley, has put the valley into cosmic perspective: "The most dramatic shape a man on the moon could see, looking our way on a good summer afternoon at four o'clock . . . would be Owens Valley." Summit climbers able to tear their eyes away from this awesome trench can spot Mount Whitney thirty-two miles to the south; its distinctive sloping summit is visible immediately right of closer, multisummited Mount Williamson. To their right lie the jagged crags of that noteworthy east-west barrier, the Kings-Kern Divide. In the opposite direction, all the significant Sierra peaks as far north as the Goddard Divide loom against the sky.

Middle Palisade

Adventurous High Route hikers who are proficient on class 3 terrain will find Middle Palisade a rewarding ascent. Leave the Muir Trail when approaching the lower Palisade Lake and ascend 2,000 feet of class 2 slabs and talus, aiming for the third chute left of the junction of Middle Palisade and its conspicuous southeastern spur. (Count the chute in the corner as the first.) Scramble up this steep, loose gully until it becomes steeper and more difficult, approximately three-fourths of the way to the summit ridge. Exit left in this vicinity and wander up a complex system of ledges and gullies until meeting the summit ridge. Care must be taken on this upper section, for the class 3 terrain is loose and exposed.

Mount Sill

In his guide to the John Muir Trail, Walter Starr Jr. regarded Mount Sill as "the peer of all Sierra peaks in the extent and quality of the views it offers." (Although Starr misused the word "peer" in this phrase, one easily grasps his meaning.) Generations of climbers have marveled at the unbelievable array of peaks stretching the ninety miles between Mounts Ritter and Whitney. Although the class 2 ascent has become popular nowadays, Mount Sill was once a rarely visited peak. After the LeConte-Hutchinson party made the first ascent in 1903, not a single person ventured onto the summit for twenty-two years, a curious fate for a lofty peak easily visible from the nearby Owens Valley. The ascent of the peak can be accomplished in a few

hours from Lake 11,672, that austere body of water covering the basin between Cirque and Potluck Passes. Ascend easy terrain north
of the lake until it becomes possible to enter a steep-sided cirque on
the left. Work up this cirque, which contains talus and steep snow, to
the ridgecrest above. The summit is then a short scramble to the east.

North Palisade

At 14,242 feet, North Palisade is the highest mountain the High Route
traveler sees at close range. For this reason alone, the ascent is a rewarding one. Only mountaineers absolutely at ease on loose class 3
terrain should attempt the ascent up the southwest face, the original—
and easiest—route. Leave the High Route east of the largest Barrett
Lake and ascend a tedious talus slope toward the huge chute that
drops from the U-Notch, the deepest notch visible to the right of the
summit. Scramble up this chute until about halfway to the U-Notch.
There, at a subtle widening of the chute, the climber stands atop a
bare-bottomed section of the gully. Nearby, on the left, is a narrow
ledge curving around the corner. Follow this sloping shelf into the
next chute and ascend it until the difficulties increase significantly.
Move right into the next chute and scramble up steep rock to the
summit ridge. The top lies just to the left. As one might expect,
the panorama from this lofty peak is extensive. But most interesting,
perhaps, is the immediate foreground view of the Sierra's largest body
of ice, the Palisade Glacier. Complete with bergschrunds and icy couloirs, this feature adds immensely to the alpine charm of the region.

Columbine Peak

High Route hikers unwilling to tackle the loose class 3 rock of the
14,000-foot crags of the Palisades should consider ascending Columbine Peak. The jagged ridge of talus rising above Knapsack Pass
proves to be a straightforward class 2 ascent. Because of its isolated
position, the 12,652-foot mass offers superb views of the Black Divide,
LeConte Canyon, and, of course, the nearby Palisades.

Mount Agassiz

Another easy peak available to High Route hikers is 13,891-foot
Mount Agassiz. Although the ascent up its western flank from Bishop
Pass involves nearly 2,000 feet of talus, the patient climber is rewarded
with a stunning view of North Palisade's convoluted topography.

Chapter Three

WHITEBARK COUNTRY
DUSY BASIN TO LAKE ITALY

Many large lakes lie in the basin's trough, some few bright with limpid water, others glittering with snow and little icebergs; others still dull with a thick coating of ice that the long siege of the midsummer day's sun is incapable of dissipating. Such is the birthplace of the San Joaquin; such the origin of that river which turns a hundred mills, irrigates a million acres of grain, fruit, and vine, and which imparts fertility and beauty to the largest and richest of California's valleys. The Sierra crest is nowhere grander, and nowhere more generous is the recompense that awaits the wearied traveller, than here among the sources of the . . . San Joaquin.

— Theodore Solomons,
from the January 1896 issue of *Appalachia*

The traveler who successfully negotiates the forty-odd miles comprising the second segment of the High Route passes through some of the most striking timberline country of the High Sierra. This adventure begins dramatically, for the hiker drops abruptly from the subalpine landscape of Dusy Basin into LeConte Canyon, a heavily wooded valley surrounded by towering granite formations. The traveler then follows the Muir Trail up this curving canyon until finally topping the Goddard Divide at Muir Pass, here forsaking the

Kings River watershed in favor of the vast region drained by the San Joaquin River. During the next ninety miles—all the way to the border of Yosemite National Park—the High Route weaves its way past the headwaters of the numerous tributaries and forks of this tumultuous river.

From Muir Pass the hiker follows the Muir Trail into Evolution Basin, a glacier-scoured trench graced with some of the most attractive lakes in the range. Eschewing the trail, the High Route next crosses the Glacier Divide at rugged, historic Snow-Tongue Pass. Remaining fairly close to the Sierra crest, the route continues over hill and dale to Bear Lakes Basin, a lovely and unspoiled region containing numerous lakes named in honor of those ursine denizens of the foothills. Lake Italy, the northern terminus of this section of the High Route, lies not far beyond.

The peaks and lake basins along this segment prove spectacular, but the flora along the way is fascinating also. From long distances the hiker can trace the course of streams by the pale green willows that line them. Wildflowers blanket acres of meadowlands, adding to the charm. The conifers, too, are well worth studying, especially in LeConte Canyon, where several species share trailside habitats. Higher, in the timberline country traversed by most of this segment of the High Route, one tree dominates: the whitebark pine.

Campsite, with a lenticular cloud hovering above the Sierra crest

Pinus albicaulis occupies a special place in the hearts of many Sierra travelers, for more than any other tree, it is the symbol of the subalpine landscape. Absent below 10,000 feet, the pine seems to seek out spectacular and lonely locations—like many backpackers. The conifer occasionally appears as an upright, normal-looking pine, but far more often it has been so harassed by the elements that it resembles a shrub; indeed, its former common name was dwarf pine. John Muir regarded the whitebark as a "tree-mountaineer that climbs highest and braves the coldest blast." The naturalist discovered that even though the contorted trees are pitifully small, they can be long-lived: one specimen, only six inches in diameter, proved to be 426 years old.

An excellent locale in which to examine the shrublike form of *albicaulis* is Mesa Lake, where it is the only pine species present. On the rocky shelves north of this remote Humphreys Basin lake, gnarled specimens appear in dense thickets. Standing in proximity to these wind-ravaged evergreens, the traveler can appreciate these words of Muir: "During stormy nights I have often camped snugly beneath the interlacing arches of this little pine. The needles, which have accumulated for centuries, make fine beds, a fact well known to other mountaineers, such as deer and wild sheep, who paw out oval hollows and lie beneath the larger trees in safe and comfortable concealment."

The whitebark pine can be recognized in two ways: by its soft-to-the-touch needles, which grow in clusters of five, and by the absence of fallen cones beneath the tree. The small cones, firmly attached to the upper branches, either disintegrate quickly on the tree when mature or are discovered by Clark's nutcrackers and chickarees—both species often are seen noisily ripping apart the cones to partake of the delectable seeds inside.

APPROACHES

Dusy Basin, the southern terminus of this section of the High Route, can be reached quite easily from the east via the Bishop Pass Trail, which leaves civilization at South Lake, a half-hour drive from Bishop. The eight-mile trail to the basin traverses splendid, lake-dotted country, and acclimated hikers will have no trouble reaching the High Route in one day's time.

Echo Col offers the hiker a strenuous, but direct, method of intersecting the High Route near Muir Pass. This route, beginning from Lake Sabrina on the Middle Fork of Bishop Creek, follows a well-worn exposure is enormous, and only those adventurers familiar with airy class 3-4 rock should attempt it.

Peak 12,971

Some peaks are reached so easily from the High Route that they should not be missed. One such is Peak 12,971 (12,920+ on the Mount Darwin quad), a Glacier Divide summit south of Snow-Tongue Pass. The class 2 talus ridge takes less than an hour from the pass, and the views from the top of the peak are stupendous. Mount Humphreys, less than five miles distant, stands etched unforgettably against the sky, its steep flanks plunging into barren Humphreys Basin. To the southeast rise the soaring summits of the Evolution group; pre-eminent is Mount Darwin, recognized by the shimmering glacier reposing under its great north face.

Mount Humphreys

Every Sierra mountaineer hopes someday to stand atop mighty Mount Humphreys. Unlike most peaks in the Sierra, this 13,986-foot colossus proves spectacular from every vantage point. And, as one might expect, such a towering formation has no truly easy route. Indeed, the final section of the standard route is steep and exposed, and though the class 4 climbing is not particularly difficult, a rope should be carried and used. The difficult section of Mount Humphreys is so short—perhaps 100 feet—and is composed of such solid rock, that its ascent seems eminently suitable for adventurous High Route mountaineers, provided, of course, there is a leader who knows how to belay properly. The southwest base of the peak is reached easily from the High Route by any one of numerous cross-country routes across Humphreys Basin. Start climbing the actual peak via a conspicuous gully that slices up on a left diagonal and across the face to the large notch just left of the summit pyramid. This gap marks the high point reached by Joseph N. LeConte and Clarence Cory on their 1898 attempt. Feeling "utterly overpowered" by the steep cliffs above the notch, the two men retreated. At this stage of his mountaineering career LeConte probably was too inexperienced to appreciate two elementary facts: frontal views distort the true steepness, and, from a distance, one cannot possibly predict the size and character of the handholds and footholds.

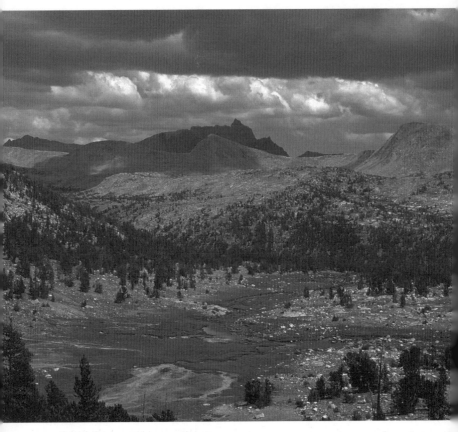

Mount Humphreys from Merriam Lake

The first complete ascent of this route didn't take place until 1919, when climbing-party leader George Bunn seemed equally impressed as LeConte with the final tower. In a *Sierra Club Bulletin* article he wrote, "A rocky depression indented the main ridge toward the summit, but this grew rapidly steeper until . . . it was so perpendicular that it leaned over backward." The Bunn party decided to investigate the route at close range, "hoping to solve each difficulty as it presented itself." By using what Bunn termed "sheer muscular power," the group attained the summit in short order.

The depression described by Bunn can be recognized immediately by the present-day climber. Scramble up this ever-steepening trough until forced to the right on narrow ledges, then climb a steep rib to the easier ground immediately below the summit. Most climbers will wish to break out the rope near the top of the trough and belay each other until close to the summit.

Virtually every major peak of the High Sierra is visible from Humphreys' minuscule summit. If the day is clear the climber can discern Mount Whitney, fifty miles to the south. In the opposite direction, forty miles distant, rise the distinctive outlines of Mount Ritter and Banner Peak. The precipitous dropoff on the northeast side of the peak is perhaps the single most impressive sight, for the Owens Valley, dominated by the town of Bishop, lies an unbelievable 9,800 feet below.

Pilot Knob
Pilot Knob, the symmetrical hulk five miles west of Mount Humphreys, provides another fine vantage point, one far more easily reached than its striking neighbor. The upper part of the 12,245-foot peak is a simple scramble from the prominent saddle to the east. This gap can be reached from the High Route in less than an hour by approaching from either Mesa or Puppet Lakes.

Feather Peak
One of the most rewarding summits attainable from the High Route is Feather Peak. Climbed and named in 1933 by David Brower, it is designated on the old map simply as Peak 13,242. Lying three-quarters of a mile northwest of Royce Peak, the mountain can be ascended from the High Route at Feather Pass by means of its classically delineated southwest ridge. The trekker must deviate from this ridge occasionally to keep the level of difficulty down to class 3. The climbing is continuous and moderately exposed, factors which contribute to a thrilling adventure.

Seven Gables
First climbed in 1894 by Theodore Solomons and Leigh Bierce, Seven Gables has long been praised as one of the range's grandest viewpoints. Solomons, in the *Sierra Club Bulletin,* was the first to exult about it: "I was too awed to shout. The ideas represented by such words as lovely, beautiful, wild or terrible, cold or desolate, fail to compass it. Words are puny things, and the language of description quite as impotent as the painter's brush. Roughly speaking, one might say that the sight was sublime and awful." Solomons, fascinated with the

splendid austerity visible below, could "fancy several hotels—perish the thought—pitched in the glacial valley. . . . The most-used path of the many that are to lead from these Swiss-like edifices will ascend the Seven Gables, and the register in the monumental cairn built on its summit will be filled with eulogies scrawled in all languages." Mercifully, no hotels or huts presently mar the view, and the thousands of hikers who have signed the register have all traveled from campsites to do so.

Other mountaineers have been equally impressed with the view from Seven Gables. In 1898 Joseph N. LeConte remained on the summit for many hours, "gazing at the wonderful panorama," and in the 1921 issue of the *Sierra Club Bulletin,* Francis Farquhar listed nearly twenty prominent summits—from Mount Lyell to Mount Whitney— visible from the 13,075-foot peak.

The superlative viewpoint can be reached quite easily from the High Route. Leave the route at Ursa Lake and follow a brook downstream to its junction with the East Fork of Bear Creek. From here ascend a 1,500-foot talus slope (often covered with snow until early August) to the prominent saddle between double-summited Seven Gables and its dramatic northern satellite. A class 2 ridge then leads south to the summit.

Chapter Four

LAKE COUNTRY
LAKE ITALY TO DEVIL'S POSTPILE

I have sometimes been asked what charm there can be in the higher levels of the Sierra, when the forests are gone and nothing remains that is not dead and forbidding, the bare crags and the snow-fields. To such a question the surest answer would be an evening spent in such a camp as we had that night. Such a scene! —wild, desolate, cold, forbidding, fascinating! White granite for miles, black shadows in the cañons and clefts, glistening snow, and tiny lakes sparkling in the moonlight; jagged, fantastic peaks and pinnacles with alpine intensity of light and shadow, and masses of ice and snow clinging to the gentler slopes. And withal the intense quiet and loneliness of the place, a seeming new world on a new planet where man and his works are as nothing. The thrill of it all comes even now, though months have passed, and will remain through the years to come.

—Lincoln Hutchinson,
from the February 1903 issue of the *Sierra Club Bulletin*

Even though the central portion of the High Route negotiates two major east-west ridges—the Mono and Silver divides—it still remains the easiest of the five segments. With only a few challenging sections, the segment extending from Lake Italy northward to Devil's Postpile traverses a magnificent landscape blessed with an inordinate share of gentle granite slabs and flower-strewn meadow-lands. True, hikers must clamber over talus blocks from time to time, but such terrain rarely persists more than a few hundred yards.

Leaving Lake Italy behind, the backpacker ascends remarkably pleasant slabs to Gabbot Pass, the last location above 12,000 feet on the High Route. Soon the hiker strolls through the Second Recess, where a dense coniferous forest comprises the most luxuriant setting since LeConte Canyon. Crossing Mono Creek at 8,500 feet, the High Route immediately surmounts the formidable north wall of the canyon. Once this obstacle is overcome, the hiker climbs up delightful countryside to the Silver Divide, the watershed boundary between the South and Middle Forks of the San Joaquin River. Not far north of here, the route follows the Muir Trail for six miles in order to circumvent a rugged, undistinguished section close to the crest. The final portion of this segment of the High Route follows the main crestline along Mammoth Crest before dropping precipitously to the Middle Fork at Devil's Postpile.

Since the countryside surrounding both the Mono and Silver Divides appears to be more rugged than it actually is, the early explorers shunned the main crest and its two great spurs in favor of the less complex country to the west, where the South Fork of the San Joaquin River afforded an obvious thoroughfare toward the prominent peaks of the Evolution group and the Goddard Divide. Nevertheless, the main watersheds of the region became fairly well known during the last one-third of the nineteenth century. In 1864 members of the California Geological Survey crossed the range at Mono Pass and descended Mono Creek westward. But this group reached only one minor summit, and the map that resulted from their labors displayed numerous blank areas. Thirty-one years later, Theodore Solomons spent several days in the environs of Mono Creek, exploring the curious U-shaped trenches he called "recesses." Like his predecessors, Solomons usually avoided the summits, preferring instead to travel along the many branches of the San Joaquin.

At last, during the ten-year period from 1898 to 1908, the heart of the area became thoroughly known. Joseph N. LeConte and James Hutchinson, those ubiquitous Sierra explorers, ascended the region's highest summits, from which they named features and mapped the countryside. Three passes, now integral components of the High Route, were first visited by one or both of these pioneers. Bighorn and Shout-of-Relief Passes were crossed by Hutchinson in 1902, shortly after he and two companions had made the first ascent of nearby Red and White Mountain. Gabbot Pass, the key to crossing the upper

Mono Divide, was reached by Hutchinson and LeConte in 1908; the latter noted that the pass would provide "a great cut-off in the High Mountain Route," which at that time circumvented the Mono Divide in the lowlands far to the west.

After the pioneers had examined every cirque and most mountain-tops, the area became frequented by curious hikers who wished to see the scenery so extolled by LeConte, Hutchinson, and their cohorts. These newcomers climbed the minor peaks, fished the creeks that churn down the enormous canyons, and camped beside the numerous—and particularly lovely—lakes dotting the landscape.

Although the High Route wends its way past hundreds of magnificent lakes during its 195-mile journey, this central segment seems to harbor a disproportionate share of the most attractive ones. Indeed, several of these lakes fulfill all the prerequisites for entering a "perfect mountain lake" contest. Such a lake displays several bottomless deeps where venerable trout—traditionally uncatchable—arrogantly flash their brilliant colors. Nearby, superimposed on a shallow underwater bench, fingerlings dart across the current-sculpted sand. Multicolored granite cliffs plunge into the blue; a few hundred feet away, however, lush meadows border sandy beaches. Both the inlet and the outlet streams vie for attention, and, in the distance, beyond the lakeshore's wonderfully twisted pines, serrated peaks dominate the horizon.

Which lake is the most sublime in this region? Is it Lower Mills Creek Lake, Laurel Lake, or one of the lovely ponds dotting the basin north of Shout-of-Relief Pass? Could the winner be the largest of the Deer Lakes? Or might it be some unnamed body of water a few hundred yards from the High Route, a place visited by only a handful of adventurers? Travelers will surely agree that no single lake wins the contest; many share first place.

APPROACHES

Lake Italy, the southern terminus of this segment of the High Route, can be reached from the east via the Italy Pass Trail. This ten-mile path, not maintained and in wretched condition above timberline, involves an elevation gain of 5,000 feet. It begins from the pack station below the Pine Creek Tungsten Mill, a mining complex reached

Descending a typical High Route slab

by a paved road leaving U.S. Highway 395 not far north of Bishop. The path branches off the more popular Pine Creek Pass Trail near Honeymoon Lake.

Another way to reach the Lake Italy region from the east is from Little Lakes Valley, at the end of the Rock Creek Road. Hike south along the valley until reaching Dade Lake. Then head southwest and climb to the first pass northwest of Bear Creek Spire. From this class 2 pass (at 13,000 feet) drop down and then contour northwest to join the High Route near Gabbott Pass.

Lake Italy can also be reached from the western flank of the Sierra. From the end of a spur road a few miles south of the dam at Lake Edison, follow the Bear Creek Trail east nearly eight miles to the Muir Trail. Follow this south two miles, then turn east and follow the path leading up the Hilgard Branch of Bear Creek. Lake Italy is reached in about five miles; the total trail distance from the roadhead is close to fifteen miles. (One can also hire a water taxi to go across Lake Edison and follow a parallel trail; this shortens the distance by four miles.)

The Mono Recesses region can be reached in a day from Lake Edison. Yet another trail to this area starts near Rock Creek Lake, climbs over the Sierra crest at Mono Pass, and descends Mono Creek until meeting the High Route at the point where it begins climbing the canyon wall north toward Laurel Lake.

Hikers who wish to join the High Route midway along this central segment can do so via the McGee Pass Trail. This scenic path crosses the Sierra crest just south of lofty Red Slate Mountain and meets the High Route at Horse Heaven, a handsome meadow at the 9,700-foot level of Fish Creek.

Devil's Postpile, the northern terminus of this portion of the High Route, is reached easily by paved road from the Mammoth Lakes region. See the "Approaches" section of Chapter 5 for details.

The longest loop trip possible in this segment is a fairly obvious one: follow the High Route all the way to Devil's Postpile, then return via the Muir Trail.

Another loop trip, shorter but more challenging than the preceding one, should appeal to hardy hikers who leave their cars near the Pine Creek Tungsten Mill. After following the High Route to the tarn-dotted basin north of Shout-of-Relief Pass, wander north a mile and intersect the McGee Pass Trail. Take this path east over the crest to Big McGee Lake, then work south over Hopkins Pass, a straightforward class 2-3 saddle. After descending easy terrain alongside Hopkins Creek, follow the trail over Mono Pass into Little Lakes Valley. At this point, pick up the path that crosses Morgan Pass and ends at the tungsten mill.

THE HIGH ROUTE

Lake Italy to Second Recess

Standing at the outlet of Lake Italy, the High Route backpacker immediately faces a dilemma: which side of the two-mile-long lake offers the easiest method of reaching Gabbot Pass? In 1908 the three pioneers who first climbed nearby Mount Abbot faced the same problem, and—with a fifty-fifty chance of choosing the easiest side—made the wrong decision. Invisible from the outlet, a half-mile-long section far along the lake's southern shore contains enormous, unstable blocks of granite. Although this side is passable, it cannot be recommended. LeConte, Hutchinson, and McDuffie returned from their climb via the northern shore; this proved trivial by comparison and is now the standard route around the lake.

Thus forewarned, the hiker should follow the northern shore of the huge lake until reaching its eastern end, where a long, surprisingly gentle slope rises to the north. Aim for Gabbot Pass, the conspicuous saddle separating massive Mount Gabb from delicate Mount Abbot. The panorama from the 12,250-foot pass proves somewhat disappointing for such an elevated vantage point, for one is hemmed in by the nearby peaks. But to the south, beyond the west shoulder of Mount Julius Caesar, towers flattopped Feather Peak, a familiar friend to those hikers who have completed the previous segment of the High Route. To the north, thirty-one miles distant, rise the twin sentinels that so dominate the northern High Sierra: Mount Ritter and Banner Peak.

The High Route in the vicinity of Gabbot Pass is cursed with an inordinate number of ducks, those piles of rock constructed by well-intentioned hikers who imagine they are the only ones capable of finding the easiest route. These ducks—distracting, unnecessary, and often misleading—spoil the sense of adventure for hikers who believe, however falsely, that they are explorers wandering across uncharted lands. It must be admitted that ducks have been around a long time; the first mention of the annoying markers in the *Sierra Club Bulletin* occurs in the June 1905 issue. Four years later, in the same journal, a brief controversy flared regarding the etymology of the word *duck*. The savants finally agreed that it derived from duckstone, a game popular in nineteenth-century England. The object of this rather mindless game was to knock off, from a distance, a small stone—the duck—that had been placed atop a larger one. Present-day High Route hikers should play this game whenever possible, until all existing ducks have vanished.

Drop down from Gabbot Pass into a gently angled valley that winds through stable talus interspersed with sandy flats. After about half a mile the hiker reaches a shallow tarn directly below the terminal moraine of the inconspicuous "rock glacier" on the north side of Mount Gabb. Finding the easiest way during the next mile requires some careful routefinding. When immediately below the tarn, bear slightly right and descend alongside a stream as it slams down a wide slot. After a short distance leave the creek and move diagonally over to a small, sandy saddle on the right. From here, pick up a path that drops down a precipitous slope into a barren valley. Walk down this path for several hundred yards to a fine viewpoint. At this point the traveler might be tempted to drop straight down to Upper Mills Creek Lake, visible below. This is indeed possible, but the easier route once again veers to the right, crossing a short, jumbled section of talus, to another barren valley. This valley eventually debouches into the

Sunset on glacier-polished slabs

meadowlands near the tarns below Upper Mills Creek Lake.

From the meadows below Upper Mills Creek Lake, follow a path down the east side of the prominent creek, reaching timberline at exquisite Lower Mills Creek Lake. The region near this lake's outlet fulfills all expectations of what a Sierra landscape should include. The creek slithers down glacier-polished slabs, drops into deep pools, then winds silently through channels etched into fragile meadows dotted with wildflowers. Stands of leaning, wind-blasted pines—some remarkably large for the elevation—are scattered across the meadowlands. In the background the steplike profile of Mount Abbot dominates the scene, especially at sundown, when for a few minutes it alone retains the alpenglow shared earlier by the other great peaks.

At some juncture the hiker must bid farewell to this idyllic place where the elements are so gracefully balanced. A path—difficult to locate at times because of downed trees—descends the north side of Mills Creek, keeping some distance from it. After about a mile the traveler arrives at the brink of an exceptionally steep slope that falls into the striking canyon known as the Second Recess. The path zigzags down this brushy, scree-covered hillside.

During this descent the hiker can enjoy an unusual Sierra sight. Across the Second Recess and about one mile distant is a gigantic, heart-shaped hole in a steep cliff. So incongruous is this feature that the mind struggles to explain it. Perhaps it is a gouge left after a massive rockfall—no, it is too deep. Perhaps it is a cave—but, no, caves don't occur in granite. All one can say is that it is a mysterious feature.

The dense forest covering the floor of the Second Recess should delight High Route trekkers, for it is the most luxuriant since LeConte Canyon. Enormous western white pines, recognized by their elongated cones, tower amid the more predominant lodgepole pines. The nearby mountains are, for once, overshadowed by the forest. A pleasant path winds down the valley, remaining close to a crystal-clear brook that meanders through meadows.

After a mile and a half of strolling through this tranquil valley, the hiker arrives at the slope that falls off into the canyon of Mono Creek. Here the observant traveler can easily absorb an elemental lesson in geology. The Second Recess, like its three neighboring recesses, is known as a hanging valley, a common feature of glaciated mountains. After a glacier has scoured a major valley, the side valleys are necessarily left suspended far above the floor of the main canyon. Thus, they terminate rather abruptly, though this depends on their size and subsequent erosion. The hiker who descends from the Second Recess is at one moment striding along the floor of a hanging valley and at the next zigzagging down the steep flank of a main valley. Hanging valleys occur throughout the Sierra, but the four Mono Recesses are prime examples of the genre, largely because of their enormous size and classic U shape.

The trail next descends through a stately forest of red firs, trees not seen on the High Route since the environs of Kings Canyon. The appearance of this ramrod-straight evergreen means that the hiker has reached the "low Sierra," for *Abies magnifica* rarely occurs above the 9,500-foot level. Cross Mono Creek on any of several fallen-log bridges and join the Mono Pass Trail on the opposite side. Follow it upstream for a third of a mile until reaching a trail junction 100 feet west of Laurel Creek. An inconspicuous sign informs the traveler that the path heading north up the slope leads to Laurel Lake.

As if to make up for the embarrassingly low elevation, the Laurel Lake Trail attacks the steep hillside with a vengeance. Eschewing switchbacks, the poorly maintained path cuts more or less straight up through dense thickets of manzanita. If the day is hot, the steepness, low elevation, and lack of shade trees make for a somewhat unpleasant hour's hike. Take heart, however, for at the 9,300-foot level several fine specimens of Jeffrey pine provide cool resting places where the traveler can gaze across Mono Creek toward the classic shape of the Second Recess. An interesting feature lies left of the entrance to this canyon, in line with massive Mount Gabb. A pale green swath slicing down the darker green of the forest indicates that an avalanche raked this slope not long ago, destroying every pine in its path. Quaking aspens now have replaced the pines, adding a welcome variation to the flora.

At last the path levels off and draws close to placid Laurel Creek, a gratifying sight to the thirsty traveler. Continue along the west bank of the creek until reaching a meadow—or bog, depending on the season—at 9,700 feet. Cross the creek here and follow a faint path through fine-looking stands of lodgepole pines. After surmounting a short headwall, the path meanders up a pleasant valley that eventually ends at Laurel Lake, a secluded timberline pond.

Leave this body of water near the two massive granite blocks adorning its northwest shore and ascend precipitous, grassy slopes

Laurel Lake, with Recess Peak in the distance

that lead upward 900 feet to Bighorn Pass, the 11,250-foot saddle immediately east of Rosy Finch Lake (the higher of two nearby notches). The nomenclature in this region is interesting. In July 1902, James Hutchinson, his brother Lincoln, and Charles Noble decided to cross this gap while returning to their camp near Cotton Lake. East of the pass, they were surprised to spy a band of twenty mountain sheep, animals the men had thought long since extinct. Tired after their first ascent of nearby Red and White Mountain, the men still managed to follow two of the agile, inquisitive beasts to the very crest of the ridge, where they vanished. The men decided to commemorate the incident by naming the lake below after the mountain sheep. But in later years their name inexplicably was transferred to the next lake to the west, and the deep rockbound body of water directly below the pass is known today as Rosy Finch Lake. But the pass itself should bear a name that is historically valid, even if the animals haven't traveled over the pass for many decades.

The view from Bighorn Pass is spectacular. Beyond Rosy Finch Lake rises the sharp silhouette of Mount Izaak Walton. Sierra historian Francis Farquhar suggested this name in 1919 to memorialize the man "to whom all fishermen and lovers of good literature are indebted for *The Compleat Angler.*" Seven miles to the south lie the four distinctive peaks that guard the upper reaches of the glacier-scooped Second Recess: Mount Abbot, huge Mount Gabb, Mount Hilgard, and truncated Recess Peak.

Bighorn Pass to Tully Hole

From the upper notch of Bighorn Pass the traveler should study the next section of the High Route, for the routefinding is a bit tricky. The next objective, a broad saddle two-thirds of a mile to the northwest, rises only a few hundred feet higher than Bighorn Pass, yet there is no easy way to contour across the labyrinthine countryside beneath the imposing cliffs of Peak 12,238 and its satellites. Do not despair. Drop down about seventy-five vertical feet from the pass, then begin clambering across rocky outcrops and short stretches of talus. Contour whenever possible, but be prepared for minor climbs and descents. There are no technical difficulties whatsoever, and the traverse from pass to pass should consume less than one hour.

When the exhausted first ascenders of Red and White Mountain reached this pass and scrutinized the gentle terrain on the opposite side, they let out a "shout of relief," according to Lincoln Hutchinson. It seems fitting that the name of this gap on the Silver Divide commemorate the emotions of the three pioneers; thus, I have termed it Shout-of-Relief Pass. The name seems doubly appropriate for this High Route pass, since the next twenty-five miles of the route pose few problems for the hiker. North of this divide, the traveler enters a region distinguished by its gentleness; rugged country will be encountered next at Nancy Pass, the gateway to the Ritter Range.

Looking north from Shout-of-Relief Pass, the traveler gazes across hundreds of square miles of mountainous terrain. Mount Ritter and Banner Peak, last seen from Gabbot Pass, now loom much more prominently; these easily recognizable masses are but two dozen miles distant. Closer to the viewer rise the clusters of unnamed summits that make up the crest region south of Mammoth Mountain. If these metamorphic hulks lack the shapeliness of other peaks in the range, at least they are far more colorful in appearance. Reds, browns, purples, buffs—all charm the jaded High Route walker accustomed to monotonously hued granite.

The pleasant and gently angled terrain dropping north of Shout-of-Relief Pass enables the hiker to reach, in short order, an open basin dotted with tarns and isolated clumps of conifers. This verdant parkland, located only a half mile from a major trail, remains remarkably untrammeled, and hikers who stroll west under the shoulder of Peak 11,411 (11,409 on the Graveyard Peak quad) toward Cotton Lake might easily envision themselves traversing meadows untrodden by human feet.

Because of its relative luxuriance, this parkland attracts a singularly complete cross-section of the breeding birds of the Sierra timberline country. Dark-eyed juncos, recognized by their small size and jet-black heads, are commonly encountered, but patient observers will see, even without binoculars, numerous other species, some of which are described below.

Mountain bluebirds flit about with abandon, radiating an ethereal sky-blue glow that contrasts vividly with the weathered wood surrounding the entrance to their nests—old woodpecker holes in dead pine snags. Yellow-rumped warblers, distinguished by the bright-yellow feathers ornamenting four parts of their bodies, fly incessantly among the pines, occasionally bursting into the sky to snare insects in a delightfully acrobatic fashion. Clark's nutcrackers, the noisiest residents of timberline country, flash distinct patches of black, gray, and white as they weave from one treetop to another during their neverending quest for pine nuts.

The sight of a Hammond's flycatcher, a fairly drab denizen of the treetops, excites the serious birder, for this species proves difficult to identify unless seen in its preferred breeding habitat, the subalpine wilderness. Ralph Hoffmann, author of *Birds of the Pacific States* (1927), relates a wry anecdote in which this tiny bird plays a role: "When Theodore Roosevelt first met John Muir, it is reported that his first question was, 'How can one tell the Hammond from the Wright Flycatcher?' It is doubtful whether any future President of the United States will have the slightest interest in the problem."

After leaving this delightful outdoor aviary, curve west past Cotton Lake to the dropoff overlooking Izaak Walton Lake, a narrow body of water reposing in a handsome setting. After working down slabs and gullies on the far left, one reaches the lake's inlet stream. Next, circle the lake on the west to the northernmost of the two outlets and descend the tree-covered benches bordering the frenzied stream, keeping west of the creek and some distance from it. After a descent of about 450 feet, the hiker will meet Fish Creek at the upper edge of Horse Heaven, a swampy meadow at the 9,700-foot level. Join the McGee Pass Trail on the opposite bank of the creek and stroll down the spectacular canyon below.

The hiker shortly encounters another enormous meadow: here, at Tully Hole, the John Muir Trail is reached. Not since Evolution Lake—some fifty trail miles to the south—has the High Route followed this famous path. But because of the complex and unattractive country near the Sierra crest, the next six miles of the High Route are concomitant with the Muir Trail. This scarcely qualifies as a hardship, however, for the countryside remains beautiful.

Tully Hole to Deer Lakes

North of Tully Hole, the Muir Trail immediately assails the steep wall of Fish Creek Canyon by means of marvelously constructed switchbacks. Soon after crossing a wooded saddle, the traveler reaches Lake Virginia, an oblong lake situated on a wide bench overlooking Cascade Valley, some 1,800 feet below.

Lovely Purple Lake is the next major landmark along the High Route; note that camping is prohibited within 300 feet of the outlet. Shortly after passing this feature, the well-graded trail curves around the southern and western flanks of Peak 11,348 (3,464 meters on the Bloody Mtn. quad). During this long traverse the hiker enjoys a wideranging view of not only Cascade Valley but the soaring peaks that make up the northwestern end of the Silver Divide.

The traveler soon reaches the marked turnoff to Duck Lake; leave the Muir Trail here and zigzag up the incline to the north. Duck Lake, the largest body of water attained by the High Route so far, makes its appearance at last. (Camping is prohibited within 300 feet of the outlet.) The lake probably was named after the waterfowl that, in late season, pause here during their migratory journey to the south.

From the lake's outlet the trail immediately begins climbing the hillside to the north. Continue for one mile to a wooded gap at 10,800 feet. Here, at Duck Pass, the High Route meets the Sierra crest for the first time. Surprisingly, the view isn't great: although Mount Ritter and

Banner Peak rise prominently to the north, few other significant peaks can be identified.

Leave the Duck Pass Trail and follow the Sierra crest west up a gentle hillside. On the whitebark-covered acres below the ridgeline, the traveler will discover thousands of obsidian chips, a sure sign that Indians once used this site to fashion their arrowheads.

A bit higher, the hiker will spot a portion of huge Mono Lake, twenty-five miles to the north. "The lonely tenant of the loneliest spot on earth," Mark Twain called it in his 1872 book, *Roughing It*. The extremely saline body of water remained relatively unknown even eighty years later, a fact that, paradoxically, almost destroyed it. Beginning in 1941 some of the water that poured into the lake from the

Tufa and clouds, Mono Lake

mountains was diverted to Los Angeles to help meet the insatiable needs of that burgeoning metropolis. By 1955 the city was taking most of the inflow and the lake's level began dropping alarmingly: by 1990 it was forty-two feet lower than it had been a half-century earlier. Nesting birds, present for millennia, faced decimation—and the lake itself seemed destined to become a sterile, dustridden bowl. Fortunately, concerned citizens and activists came to the rescue, and, after a lengthy battle, forced Los Angeles by legal means to be less rapine. Thanks to this action and several heavy winters thereafter, the lake has been rising since 1994 and should slowly continue to rise to a court-mandated level—well below the historic level but enough to preserve the lake. Wildlife will slowly come back, though who knows what long-term ecologic damage has been done. Let's hope that visitors will always be entranced by the sight of the 700,000 eared grebes that pause each autumn during migration. (For further reading on the Mono Lake story, I recommend John Hart's excellent 1996 book, *Storm Over Mono*.)

With this reminder of man's folly (and heroism) constantly in sight, continue along the fairly level main crest until reaching the low saddle to the immediate right of craggy Peak 11,647 (3,546 meters on the Bloody Mtn. quad). The view to the south from this 11,200-foot pass proves so superior to that from Duck Pass that it is hard to believe the latter lies only half a mile away and 400 feet lower. Although the upper portions of both Red Slate Mountain and Red and White Mountain are visible, the prime view is of the Mount Abbot group and Seven Gables; both massifs loom prominently.

The only long-distance view to the north is of the Clark Range, a major ridge near Yosemite Valley. In line with this isolated chain of peaks, and only a quarter of a mile distant, the hiker can distinguish another low gap on the Sierra crest. Cross the sand-covered basin to this saddle, then descend a gentle slope west for about 100 feet. There, at an abrupt dropoff, is a splendid view of the three Deer Lakes in their pleasant, inviting setting.

A good path winds down the steep talus slope, and soon the hiker arrives at the scree-covered benches above the uppermost Deer Lake. Leave the faint path near here and wander over hill and dale to the northernmost Deer Lake, an exquisite body of water ringed by slabs and meadows. Fill the water bottles here, for there's no water from here until Red's Meadows, the longest dry section on the High Route.

Deer Lakes to Mammoth Pass

Head west a few hundred feet from this lake and join the Deer Creek Trail as it assaults the hillside to the north in a rudely direct manner. After a climb of about 400 vertical feet, the traveler approaches the main Sierra crest yet again. Here, along what is called Mammoth Crest, the trail begins contouring below the ridgeline. At one point the trail passes a "window" in the crest, and from there the viewer can gaze straight down into the populated valley of Mammoth Creek; this marks the first sign of civilization along the High Route thus far.

The panorama from Mammoth Crest rivals any of the entire High Route. So isolated and high is this airy ridge that the viewer has the impression of staring at the landscape from an airplane. To the south, Mount Hilgard and its distinctive, flat-topped neighbor, Recess Peak, can be seen. Seven Gables, as always, rises spectacularly against the skyline. To its right, displaying a sheer northern escarpment, is Mount Hooper, the guardian of the Selden Pass region.

It is to the north, however, that the panorama outdoes itself. The entire Clark Range is visible, as is the dark and sinister Ritter Range. To the left of the spires comprising the Minarets—and far beyond them—rises the massive white pyramid called Foerster Peak; the traveler later will cross the pass just to its left as the High Route enters Yosemite National Park. Framed perfectly in the Ritter-Banner saddle is lofty Mount Lyell, nineteen miles distant. Farther right, the viewer can identify Donohue Peak by the parallel avalanche chutes on its south face. Closer at hand is bleak Mammoth Mountain, with its summit buildings.

Soon after leaving the highest part of Mammoth Crest the hiker begins a gradual descent through a sparse whitebark-pine forest. Later, on an extensive plateau, picturesque whitebark snags, along with healthy specimens, line the indistinct main crest like sentinels guarding against invaders from the west. The mountains on all sides seem disembodied, for their lower ramparts are hidden beneath the rim of the plateau. Because of the "floating" mountains and the primordial foreground, a mystical quality pervades this plateau, and it seems incomprehensible that one is standing atop the Sierra crest.

Follow the crestline north for another mile or so, entering along the way a zone of twisted, red lava, extremely young by geological standards. Finally, at a small knoll, the Deer Creek Trail drops inconspicuously toward Mammoth Lakes. The High Route continues along

the crest, passing several notches that overlook the by-now sheer east side of the range. After about half a mile, the traveler reaches the top of the steep dropoff overlooking Mammoth Pass, that vast gap in the main crest south of Mammoth Mountain. Steep cliffs lie below this point, so head down on a westbound diagonal to the obvious sandy saddle east of Peak 10,005 (3,054 meters on the Crystal Crag quad). Don't waste time looking for the trail indicated on the old topo map, for it does not exist, at least not in any maintained fashion. This fact proves to be no problem when going downhill, for the hiker simply can plow down the pumice-filled gully that debouches onto Mammoth Pass. The general unpleasantness of this short section is partially offset by the appearance of the delicate mountain hemlock, which soon almost totally usurps the whitebark pines. This graceful conifer, generally absent from the southern Sierra, will be seen quite often on the remainder of the High Route.

Mammoth Pass to Devil's Postpile

After the terrain levels out, the traveler continues north through a dense forest of lodgepole pines. In about 200 yards from the base of the hill one will encounter a well-used trail running east to west. Don't take this trail; instead, step across it and strike north cross-country, aiming for reddish Mammoth Mountain for 400 yards, to a second trail. Here, at 9,350 feet, is a tranquil area that almost demands that the traveler pause and contemplate the surroundings.

Although Mammoth Pass forms the lowest spot on the entire High Sierra crest, its more interesting attribute concerns its geology. Near here, eons ago, basalt surged forth from a vent and plunged into the canyon of the Middle Fork of the San Joaquin River. As explained in the following chapter, one remnant of this flow is known today as Devil's Postpile. Much more visible than the basalt, however, is the layer of pumice that blankets the entire Mammoth Pass region. Although this pumice forms only a veneer in most locations, near the pass it is estimated to be nearly 1,000 feet thick. The steam-shredded bits of siliceous lava, astonishingly light and delicate, were carried here by the wind following the explosions of the numerous small volcanoes south of Mono Lake.

Pine snag on Mammoth Crest, Mount Ritter and Banner Peak in the background

During heavy rainstorms this pumice floats eerily in the depression of the trail, causing travelers to question their eyesight at times. More frequently, however, the pumice simply annoys the hiker, for it is difficult to move efficiently through the loose, airy material. High Route trekkers become immediately aware of this fact as they head west on the trail as it begins its 1,700-foot descent to the Middle Fork.

After about two miles—during which time the traveler has entered a fine stand of red firs—a trail junction is reached not far above the canyon floor. Keep right to reach nearby Red's Meadow, with its store and pack station. (Those who wish to avoid civilization altogether, and Devil's Postpile also, are advised to take the left fork; the Muir Trail is soon met and can be followed across the San Joaquin and up the west side of the river.)

At 7,600 feet, Red's Meadow is the lowest elevation reached by the entire High Route, except for its two end points. From the store follow a path west and soon hit the main paved road leading to Mammoth Lakes. Follow this right some 500 yards and, just before crossing Red's Creek, take a marked path on the left—this leads, in less than a mile, to Devil's Postpile, the northern terminus of this segment of the High Route.

REVERSING THE ROUTE

Southbound travelers on this segment of the High Route encounter their first routefinding dilemma at Mammoth Pass, where they must locate the correct gully leading up onto Mammoth Crest. Because the flat acres constituting Mammoth Pass are blanketed with a dense stand of lodgepole pines, it proves somewhat difficult to discover a break from which to peer south. But after locating such a gap, the traveler can see, about half a mile distant, a massive bluff with steep cliffs, directly on the Sierra crest. To its right is a sandy saddle with a wide, tree-covered gully dropping from it. (On the map this gully is located directly east of Peak 10,005. The trail shown on the map does not exist.) Ascend the tedious, sandy slopes leading to the saddle, then work up the incline on the left. Soon the hiker will be striding south along Mammoth Crest.

Follow the trail along Mammoth Crest until, after several miles, it drops abruptly to the northernmost of the Deer Lakes. Leave the trail here and work east across gentle terrain until nearly at the southeastern Deer Lake; from there the traveler can spot, close at hand to the east, a conspicuous gap in the Sierra crest. A rough path zigzags up 250 feet to this 11,200-foot pass.

The hiker does not remain on the eastern side of the Sierra for long. Work east across a sand-covered flat for one-quarter of a mile to a prominent saddle that barely rises above the level of the basin. From here the traveler can easily study the gentle terrain leading down and across to Duck Pass.

Hikers should encounter no further routefinding problems until approaching the Silver Divide. The first place that may prove perplexing occurs a mile or so after leaving the Muir Trail. The hiker must leave the McGee Pass Trail near the far end of the pleasant meadow known as Horse Heaven and ascend the slope west of the stream draining Izaak Walton Lake. After passing around this narrow body of water on the west, turn hard left and surmount a short headwall to the bench on which Cotton Lake reposes. From here contour east around the shoulder of Peak 11,411 until reaching a tree-covered basin containing numerous tarns.

From the basin, work southeast toward Shout-of-Relief Pass, the gentle saddle immediately to the right of conspicuous Peak 12,238. (Avoid heading straight south from the lake basin; this route leads to a pass overlooking Bighorn Lake.) From Shout-of-Relief Pass the next mile of the High Route is visible. Contour southeast, occasionally moving up or down, underneath the spectacular cliff band shooting southeast from Peak 12,238. Bighorn Pass is the highest feasible crossing point along this ridge.

Much farther south, near the end of this segment of the High Route, the traveler comes across another possible routefinding problem: the north side of Gabbot Pass. From the large tarn below Upper Mills Creek Lake, the hiker will notice several rounded hillocks more or less in line with Gabbot Pass, the obvious gap to the right of lofty Mount Abbot. The easiest route to this saddle follows a crude path hidden in shallow valleys on the far left side of the hillocks. The path fades as the traveler approaches the saddle, but by this time the route is more than obvious.

ALTERNATE ROUTES

Because of the relative ease of this segment of the High Route, only one alternate route needs to be mentioned here. This alternate—which appears, upon studying the map, to be more practical than the High

Route—begins at Laurel Lake. Head northeast up the hillside to meet Grinnell Lake, then proceed up rocky slopes to the 11,600-foot pass immediately west of Red and White Mountain. It is now possible to descend slate-covered slopes to the meadowlands surrounding Tully Lake. This alternate, long considered to be the standard cross-country route across the Silver Divide, proves less efficient than the High Route for three reasons: it requires an extra elevation gain; it involves traversing large sections of loose slate; and, because of its geographical setting, it retains snow and even ice until September.

Mountaineering

Peaks around Lake Italy

Centrally located Lake Italy provides a good starting point for several significant summits. Monolithic Mount Hilgard can be climbed in a few hours from the lake's outlet. Mount Julius Caesar, with its striking view of well-named Lake Italy, can be reached via the loose class 2 slopes that rise above Italy Pass. Bear Creek Spire can be ascended from the head of the lake: hike up seemingly endless talus to the class 3 summit rocks, which are best approached from the north.

Mount Gabb

Gabbot Pass is the standard departure point for climbing the two peaks that give the pass its name. The northeast ridge of Mount Gabb offers the mountaineer a straightforward class 3 ascent. Instead of slavishly following the ridge, wander away from it when confronted by steep sections.

Mount Abbot

As evidenced by the following statistic, early Sierra Club members were entranced by Mount Abbot: of the thirty-eight persons who signed the summit register between 1908 and 1930, all but two were members of that then-small organization. During the following half-century, of course, that ratio was not maintained, and hundreds of mountaineers with other affiliations—or none at all—have stood atop the region's highest summit. From Gabbot Pass the route is fairly clear. Ascend a talus slope over to a wide chute on the right side of the steep buttress that diagonals down from the summit. The 200-foot cliff rising above the head of the chute provides the main challenge of the route. The steep wall can be surmounted in various places; the

Late afternoon at 11,700 feet

easiest route is class 3. Once the cliff has been climbed, the top is reached by a short stroll across the surprisingly extensive summit plateau.

Red and White Mountain

Rising from the junction of the Silver Divide with the Sierra crest, Red and White Mountain offers an interesting climb capped by a superb viewpoint. The 12,850-foot summit first was reached in 1902 by the Hutchinson brothers and Charles Noble. As the victorious trio stood at the top, they tried to conjure up a "less clumsy and more euphonious" name than Red-and-White Peak, the name bestowed by Theodore Solomons eight years earlier. Although the men knew that first ascenders traditionally could name or rename the peaks they climbed, they finally decided to retain the old name since, as Hutchinson wrote in the *Sierra Club Bulletin*, it was "peculiarly descriptive of the great peak of red slate fantastically streaked with seams of white granite." (By the time Norman Clyde made the second ascent twenty-six years later, Peak had become Mountain; mapmakers later dropped the hyphens.)

The summit can be reached by several routes, two of which leave the High Route at Laurel Lake. The first follows the upper part of the original ascent route: walk up talus to the pass between the mountain and Peak 12,238, then scramble up the loose class 3 ridge to the top. The exposure on the upper ridge proves impressive, and several places call for extra caution. First-ascender Lincoln Hutchinson recalled one of these spots in an article in the *Sierra Club Bulletin:* "Midway [up] the worst portion of this knife-edge we suddenly came to a huge block of slate set squarely athwart our course. Our route seemed absolutely blocked to any animal without wings, and for a few moments failure stared us in the face." But the intrepid pioneers soon solved the problem, as will the present-day mountaineer who recognizes this particular obstacle.

The second route on Red and White Mountain follows the route descended by the 1902 first-ascent party: climb the loose, conspicuous class 2 chute that rises above Little Grinnell Lake.

Red Slate Mountain
The gigantic red pyramid known as Red Slate Mountain totally dominates its surroundings: at 13,163 feet it is the highest crest peak in many miles. Indeed, to the north, there is no higher peak in the remaining sixty miles of the High Sierra, and to the south, the serpentine crest does not pierce the 13,000-foot level once again until it rises at the Mount Abbot group, some eight miles distant. The panorama from this colorful peak encompasses a vast region, and climbers familiar with the shapes of major Sierra peaks will be able to identify dozens of them in the seventy-mile stretch of wilderness between Mount Conness and Mount Goddard. The High Route traveler can climb this significant peak from the vicinity of Cotton Lake. Because of loose rock and a lack of challenging sections, the ascent is not particularly enjoyable, and prospective climbers might heed the words of Joseph N. LeConte, one of the first ascenders: "The jagged fragments of slate are even more trying to the patience than to the shoes."

Peak 11,348
A popular goal of day-hikers based at Mammoth Lakes, Peak 11,348 (3,462 meters on the Crystal Crag quad) certainly is worth the ten-minute effort it takes to climb it from the High Route. This inconspicuous mountain, located on Mammoth Crest midway between Duck and Mammoth Passes, provides a sterling panorama of the Mammoth Lakes region and the Ritter Range.

Chapter Five

HEADWATERS COUNTRY
DEVIL'S POSTPILE TO TUOLUMNE MEADOWS

Now came the solemn, silent evening. Long, blue, spiky shadows crept out across the snow-fields, while a rosy glow, at first scarce discernible, gradually deepened and suffused every mountain-top, flushing the glaciers and the harsh crags above them. This was the alpenglow, to me one of the most impressive of all the terrestrial manifestations of God. At the touch of this divine light, the mountains seemed to kindle to a rapt, religious consciousness, and stood hushed and waiting like devout worshippers. Just before the alpenglow began to fade, two crimson clouds came streaming across the summit like wings of flame, rendering the sublime scene yet more impressive; then came darkness and the stars.

—John Muir, *The Mountains of California*, 1894

The High Route traveler may well become uneasy when surrounded by the multitudes of tourists and backpackers who cluster around the road's end near Devil's Postpile. Fortunately, he or she soon will be alone again, wandering through the spectacular wilderness that surrounds the headwaters of four major Sierra rivers: the Middle and North Forks of the San Joaquin, the Merced, and the Tuolumne.

For the first few days of this segment of the High Route, the hiker traverses the sublime country lying beneath the glacier-clad faces of the Minarets and the twin sentinels of the northern High Sierra, Mount Ritter and Banner Peak. Fishermen, climbers, and families long ago discovered the delights of this easily accessible flank of the Ritter Range, and in August people flock to the most popular locations. The majority of these wilderness lovers stick closely to the established trails, which leave the Muir Trail every few miles and ascend gentle valleys toward the lakes nestled under serrated peaks. Yet this region proves eminently suited to the traveler who prefers cross-country travel. For example, the pleasant, trailless High Route traverse from Superior Lake to Thousand Island Lake offers easy walking with only several rough sections. Elevation differences on this seven-mile jaunt never exceed 900 feet at any one place, a relief to those hikers weary of more extreme ups and downs. Still, one shouldn't take this segment lightly, for talus, loose gullies, and steep, north-facing snowfields must be overcome during the traverse under the Minarets. Those who feel uneasy on such terrain are advised to begin the segment at Thousand Island Lake.

High Route trekkers interested in geology will especially appreciate the initial part of this segment, for the Ritter Range provides colorful and convoluted topography. François Matthes, the famed geologist of the Sierra Nevada, once noted the geological significance of the region: "When you climb Mount Ritter, you climb the core of one of the ancestral mountains that were formed more than a hundred million years before the present Sierra Nevada was uplifted." Josiah Whitney, leader of the California Geological Survey in the 1860s, stated that the rock of the Ritter Range was granite, but the learned scientist was in error. The mottled, dark gray rock is actually ancient lava that has been greatly metamorphosed.

At Glacier Lake Pass, the watershed boundary between the San Joaquin River's Middle and North Forks, the traveler stands on the threshold of a region so rarely visited that for the following days it is easy to imagine being the first to explore the slabs and meadowlands. And, indeed, there is a scarcity of information about the original explorations around the headwaters of the North Fork. Theodore Solomons, whose peregrinations farther south are documented elsewhere in this book, wandered through this wild region in 1897, when for the third time he stood atop Mount Ritter. Since this ascent was

The Minarets from Cecile Lake

made from the headwaters of the Merced River, Solomons must have crossed the North Fork of the San Joaquin; alas, his itinerary is not known.

Blue Lake Pass, the High Route saddle south of Foerster Peak, was first crossed in 1907 when a group of fifteen adventurers from that year's Sierra Club outing made the journey from the headwaters of the Merced River to Thousand Island Lake. Other Sierra Club parties traversed the identical route in subsequent years. Later, Walter Starr Jr. briefly described the cross-country trek in his well-known trail guide, concluding his somewhat vague account with a succinct and accurate statement: "This is a fairly rough but short and spectacular route for knapsackers."

Straightforward cross-country travel between Blue Lake Pass and Tuolumne Meadows proves impossible because of the Mount Lyell group's radiating western ridges, most of which harbor steep, snowy north sides unpleasant and even dangerous to the backpacker. Thus, the final days of this segment of the High Route involve hiking along infrequently traveled trails in the backcountry of Yosemite National Park. As one approaches the commercial camp near Vogelsang Lake—seven miles south of Tuolumne Meadows—hordes of hikers appear once again, a sure indication that a road lies nearby.

APPROACHES

Devil's Postpile National Monument, the southern terminus of this segment of the High Route, lies near the end of a paved road that leaves U.S. Highway 395 and crosses the Sierra crest just north of that downhill skier's paradise, Mammoth Mountain. Summer visitors must park at the ski area and take a shuttle bus ($7 round trip in 1997) over the crest and down to Devil's Postpile. This efficient system, inaugurated in the summer of 1979 by the U.S. Forest Service, greatly relieves traffic congestion along the narrow road that descends to the Middle Fork of the San Joaquin River. The shuttle is mandatory during the summer, but optional during the early fall months.

The northern terminus of this section of the High Route is Tuolumne Meadows, a well-known attraction on the trans-Sierra road that crosses Tioga Pass. This strikingly beautiful region offers the visitor a store, gas station, and ranger station, as well as an enormous campground.

An appealing loop trip can alleviate transportation problems for those hikers who leave their cars at Mammoth. Leave the High Route at the Vogelsang High Sierra Camp and follow the trail that heads east past Evelyn Lake to meet the Muir Trail in Lyell Canyon. From this junction twenty-one miles of relatively easy walking leads to the shuttle-bus stop at Agnew Meadows.

THE HIGH ROUTE

Devil's Postpile to Minaret Lake

The famed geological wonder known as Devil's Postpile is worth examining in some detail, for it is one of the finest North American examples of columnar basalt. Many of its sixty-foot columns rise straight as an arrow; others curve sensuously. Those who take the time to visit the top of the formation will be pleasantly surprised, for glaciers have burnished the severed tops of the columns, forming a charming mosaic.

Curious trekkers may wonder about the origin of the formation. Several hundred thousand years ago, a gigantic flow of black basaltic lava spewed forth from a fissure near present-day Mammoth Pass. After covering the canyon floor to a depth of about 500 feet, the cooling basalt contracted into columns. Most of these columns had either five or six sides, but some were formed with three, four, seven, or eight sides. Tens of thousands of years later, the so-called Middle

Fork Glacier steadily carried away most of the region's basalt, leaving only scattered, unyielding outcrops—like the Postpile—for modern visitors to appreciate.

Sheepherders were responsible for naming this geological curiosity. According to an 1894 report by Theodore Solomons, "in every scenic freak the sheepherder recognizes the handiwork of his Satanic majesty. This formation is therefore known to local fame as the Devil's Woodpile." By 1911, when the national monument was established, the name had evolved into its present form.

Hikers starting the northbound High Route from this area leave civilization at the Devil's Postpile parking lot and stroll south toward the feature for about 250 yards. A trail then crosses the Middle Fork of the San Joaquin River on a narrow footbridge. Ascending gently upward, the path skirts minor basaltic remnants, black and angular. The blindingly white pumice of the Mammoth Mountain region blankets the ground, making the hiking less than pleasant. About half a mile from the bridge the traveler meets the dusty Muir Trail. Follow this right (in the direction of Minaret Lake and Shadow Lake) as it ascends for about three-quarters of a mile to the Beck Lakes Trail, which comes in from the left, soon after one has passed the gorge containing hidden Minaret Falls. Bid farewell to the Muir Trail; the High Route will follow it for only one more mile, many days hence.

Ascend the Beck Lakes Trail as it switchbacks up a hillside covered with splendid examples of western white pine, mountain hemlock, and red fir. Five miles west of the river the trail drops 200 feet into the King Creek drainage. Not far beyond lies Superior Lake, a beautiful body of water marred somewhat by overdeveloped shoreline campsites. During the seven miles from Devil's Postpile, the traveler has gained slightly more than 2,000 vertical feet. Free at last from the huge canyon of the Middle Fork, the hiker stands again at the gateway to timberline country.

From the west end of Superior Lake continue west along the path. Almost immediately the traveler enters the finest stand of mountain hemlocks on the entire High Route. Small purple cones, cylindrical in shape, grow in profusion throughout the upper half of the tree; in late season thousands of fallen cones, as delicate as the conifer itself, blanket the ground. It is easy to see why John Muir called the hemlock "the very loveliest tree in the forest."

Leaving this idyllic place about a quarter of a mile beyond Superior Lake, the High Route begins ascending a 600-foot slope that ends at 10,200-foot Nancy Pass, the conspicuous gap west of Peak 10,532 (Red Top Mountain on the Mount Ritter quad). The view from this pass is the finest seen from the High Route since Mammoth Crest. Red Slate Mountain, displaying a distinctive snow couloir, rises prominently to the south; less identifiable is the Mount Abbot group, but to its right is the sharp outline of that familiar High Route peak, Seven Gables. The panorama to the north proves far more interesting, for the peaks are intimate and colorful. The southern spires of the Minarets loom close at hand, and Mount Ritter and Banner Peak dominate the background. A minuscule portion of Minaret Lake—the next major High Route landmark—is visible below massive Volcanic Ridge. The route toward the lake should be studied carefully from Nancy Pass, for it is a bit tricky. Avoid descending to the meadowlands directly below; instead the object is to travel on a diagonal down and to the left, losing as little elevation as possible.

Descend unstable talus below Nancy Pass, then wander left toward the uppermost visible trees. From here drop down a precipitous slope to easier ground, then contour to the north. Pass over the inconspicuous saddle west of Peak 9,833 (3,004 meters on the Mt. Ritter quad) and descend into the lush meadowlands below Deadhorse Lake. An imposing, dark horn of rock interrupts the skyline to the north: this is the first of the Minarets, Riegelhuth Minaret. Contour north under this striking formation to the southeast shore of Minaret Lake.

For more than half a century this beautifully situated lake has been a favorite base camp for mountaineering activities, and it is easy to see why. Triangular Clyde Minaret dominates the skyline above the far side of the lake. First climbed in 1928 by the legendary Norman Clyde, the 12,281-foot dagger, highest of the Minarets, offers the competent rock climber half a dozen routes, including one so excellent it was included in the book *Fifty Classic Climbs of North America* by the author and Allen Steck. This demanding ascent, first accomplished in 1963 by Steck and others, lies near the center of the face as viewed from the lake.

From the same side of the lake the hiker can spy Michael Minaret, the second-highest pinnacle of the Minarets, peeking out from behind the left-hand skyline of Clyde. This remote, needlelike pinnacle, invisible from most viewpoints, occupies a sacred niche in the range's mountaineering history. It was here, close to the peak's summit, that Walter Starr Jr. fell to his death while solo climbing in August 1933. His body, discovered weeks later by Norman Clyde, was entombed on the ledge where it was found.

Other climbers have been killed or injured while seeking these airy summits, and inexperienced persons tempted to scale the heights should heed these words of Charles Michael, a famous solo climber of the 1920s: "There is no friendliness about the Minarets. When seen from a distance they wear a black and sinister look. Precipitous walls rise to the sky-line, where beetling crags cut raggedly against the horizon. There are no gentle slopes to beckon one to the summit; rather does the scowling sheerness warn one off. The spirit of the mountain is the spirit of defiance. . . . "

Minaret Lake to Whitebark Pass

After absorbing the sterling view, the High Route hiker must reach the western shore of 9,800-foot Minaret Lake. After midseason this is done most easily by traversing the south shore; in early season a massive snowbank drops directly into the lake and bars easy progress, especially in the morning, when the snow can be rock hard. It takes only twenty minutes longer to wind around the lake on its north side; at the outlet the traveler passes the unmarked western terminus of the Minaret Lake Trail, which leads six miles east to join the Muir Trail.

From the west side of Minaret Lake ascend a rough path up the north side of the creek that is seen foaming above. Aim for the right side of the broad saddle forming the "dam" of Cecile Lake, the next higher body of water. Leave the creek when it veers toward Clyde Minaret and ascend a faint path through talus and grass to a short class 3 slot that slices through a steep cliff band; the 10,240-foot lake lies just beyond.

Traverse easy talus and slabs around the east and north shores of austere Cecile Lake to its outlet, a marvelous juxtaposition of water and metamorphic rock. From here the hiker has an excellent view of the main Minaret Ridge. Clyde Minaret appears more ridgelike than needlelike now; it was on the steep wall above a pocket-sized glacier that Norman Clyde made his solo first ascent. To the north is a super view of Ritter and Banner; this is the final time the traveler can take in the "traditional" view visible for so long on the High Route. Directly below Cecile Lake lies Iceberg Lake, a body of water so sheltered from the summer's sun that it remains free of ice only three or four months a year.

From the outlet of Cecile Lake follow a path down a steep, unpleasant slope high above the eastern shore of Iceberg Lake. The diagonal descent usually involves crossing a major snowfield or two, but often there are footsteps in the snow, making the passage easier. Here's where a ski pole or a stick is a godsend. (Don't do this section before mid-afternoon if the snow is hard—and don't get too close to the lake on this traverse: the snowfield is horrifyingly undercut in places.)

The hiker eventually meets the lake at its outlet, a singularly peaceful place. From here follow a prominent path north toward Ediza Lake. After about 125 yards leave the trail and cross the creek to the obvious path on the opposite side. Continue along a wooded bench for about 400 yards to a gap that offers a fine viewpoint of the next section of the High Route. The object of the next few hours is to gain the high meadowlands below the Ritter-Banner saddle. The going through the hemlock forest is fairly straightforward; higher, a nice path winds upward on the north side of the main creek.

Upon reaching a bleak tarn at the 10,050-foot level, close to the giant peaks above, the High Route abruptly changes direction, ascending a gentle incline northeast toward the Nydiver Lakes. As soon as the first of these lakes is spotted, begin contouring diagonally over toward hidden Whitebark Pass, recognized by the two tiny clumps of pines not far below it. (On the map it's the wide saddle immediately west of Peak 10,704—3,258 meters on the Mt. Ritter quad.) Just before reaching this pass, the traveler will come across a superb specimen of whitebark pine, its ancient trunk seemingly welded to the rock.

At Whitebark Pass the hiker stands astride the divide separating Shadow Creek from Garnet Lake, now visible below. A glance back to the south proves rewarding, for the serrated Minarets tower dramatically above the visible portions of Cecile and Iceberg Lakes.

Whitebark Pass to Glacier Lake Pass

On the north side of Whitebark Pass a steep snowfield lingers most of the year; do not attempt to descend this! Instead, move about 100 feet to the east, where a steep and loose defile plunges 100 feet before debouching onto a talus slope or a short snowfield. Clamber down this section (if the snow is hard, be extremely careful) to the meadowlands west of the lakes that lie above the head of Garnet Lake.

A gentle stroll to the north soon takes the High Route hiker to yet another watershed boundary, this one a 10,175-foot saddle overlooking the vast expanse of Thousand Island Lake. Whether or not 1,000

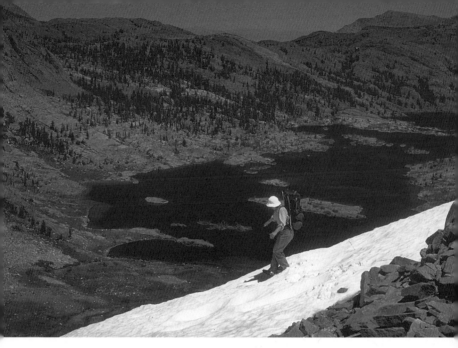

Glissading below Whitebark Pass, with Garnet Lake in the background

islands actually exist proves immaterial, for the name eloquently conveys the idea. No other Sierra lake is so dotted with islands as this mile-and-a-half-long body of water. On a trip in 1892, Theodore Solomons became intrigued by the scenic wonder, calling it—and its environs—"an almost ideal Alpine landscape. One unconsciously looks along the shore of the lake for the ubiquitous Swiss Hotel."

Easy walking from the pass leads down to the tree-covered isthmus that lies between the lake and the three ponds to its left. In midseason the meadows in this area display numerous varieties of wildflowers, with paintbrush predominating. Contrasting vividly with such luxuriance is the somber façade of Banner Peak, exactly 3,000 feet above.

From the far side of the isthmus continue up gentle terrain in the same direction to a major stream descending from the flanks of Mount Davis. Eventually, turn west up this brook—the chief inlet stream of Thousand Island Lake—and ascend terrain speckled with solitary groves of whitebark pine. Timberline country rarely offers more pleasant walking than it does in this region, for as the traveler strides alongside the marvelously clear and turbulent creek, the nearby peaks tower dramatically overhead and lakes glimmer in the distance.

The observant hiker undoubtedly will spot several pairs of dippers, or water ouzels, along this creek, for the habitat proves absolutely perfect for this curious bird. Rarely more than inches from water—and often either partially or completely submerged—these stocky, gray denizens of Sierra waters intrigued John Muir, who once wrote a 5,000-word essay lauding them. In almost every Sierra stream, he wrote, "you will surely find its complementary Ouzel, flitting about in the spray, diving in foaming eddies, whirling like a leaf among beaten foam-bells; ever vigorous and enthusiastic, yet self-contained, and neither seeking nor shunning your company." Commenting on their cheerful disposition even in a storm, when other birds cower in abject misery, Muir found that the dippers "could no more help exhaling sweet song than a rose sweet fragrance." The neophyte birder should have no trouble identifying the dipper: its chunky form constantly bobs up and down, and, in flight, the bird skims the surface of the water, following each and every bend in the stream.

The High Route traveler next proceeds southwest up a shallow basin toward the low saddle separating Banner Peak from Mount Davis. Until late season a massive snowfield guards the final approach to the pass; but this obstacle is not particularly steep, and the hiker should reach 11,158-foot Glacier Lake Pass with little trouble. From this desolate spot (called North Glacier Pass on the Mt. Ritter quad) one gets a unique view of the sensuously shaped glacier on Mount Ritter's north side. Originating at the Banner-Ritter Col, this narrow glacier ends shortly above Lake Catherine, a rockbound lake in an austere setting devoid of vegetation.

Glacier Lake Pass to the Twin Island Lakes

Drop down from Glacier Lake Pass to the shoreline of nearby Lake Catherine and follow stable talus around the lake's north side to the flat benches at its western end. Continue west a few hundred feet to a lonely tarn, then follow the main creek south. In 100 yards the hiker arrives abruptly at a dropoff overlooking the chasm of the North Fork of the San Joaquin River. Across this awesome gorge—and only a mile and a quarter as the raven flies—the traveler can spot one of the Twin Island Lakes; the High Route soon will traverse the shores of both these remote lakes.

Below the viewpoint, a wild stream roars headlong down slabs and cliffs. In this area the backpacker must wander carefully down the class 2 ramps and ledges bordering the stream's north side. After several hundred yards of this fascinating terrain, the hiker reaches the brink of an eighty-foot waterfall that plunges into the tarn shown on the map at the 10,650-foot level (3,240 meters on the Mt. Ritter quad). Since this cliff is very steep, turn right and traverse up and across ledges on the whitish outcrop to the north. The following stage of the descent involves short class 3 cliffs that separate complex ledge systems. Hikers should consider having the most experienced person in the group reconnoiter the next section while the others wait for the verdict. Since the exposure in this area is minimal, little danger is involved; nevertheless, this section could result in anxious moments for the beginning backpacker.

Not far below this rugged section, the traveler reaches a conspicuous meadow situated several hundred feet north of the main stream. This isolated glade, perched above an alarmingly steep 400-foot cliff, offers the hiker a temporary respite from the world of stone. After peering over the cliff to check out the scenery below, backtrack into the meadow about 100 feet. Then turn due north and follow a meadowy corridor toward reddish cliffs in the distance. Continue in this direction for several hundred yards until it is possible to traverse diagonally down into the wide gully (with a stream) on the left. Many different routes may be followed in this vicinity, but all eventually meet in a pleasant meadow with a welcome grove of lodgepole and whitebark pines.

From this isolated grove of pines at 9,900 feet (3,020 meters on the Mt. Ritter quad), climb up a few feet to the north, then follow a rough path that leads 100 yards along a bench before dropping down into a loose gully. This proves to be an excellent place from which to study the route over to the Twin Island Lakes. The High Route does not descend very far into the classic, U-shaped valley of the North Fork, but rather contours around its head. Although this section is not at all difficult, it is somewhat complicated, involving numerous minor elevation changes as well as tricky routefinding through labyrinthine granite corridors.

The object is to reach the south end of the northern Twin Island Lake, and once this goal is attained, the High Route wanderer faces a dilemma not often encountered in the High Sierra: a significant river crossing. Because of the complex topography near the outlet of the lake, there is only one way to cross the infant North Fork, and that is to wade. The sound of the raging river below the outlet reminds the traveler not to falter in midstream, but the crossing proves easier than it looks; the current is sluggish, and the water is only three feet deep. The most experienced—or bravest—person in the group should take charge and ferry the others' packs across the twenty-foot-wide obstruction.

With this minor hindrance behind, the backpacker ascends a gentle slope that levels out near the north end of the southern Twin Island Lake. Turn this infrequently visited body of water on the left by means of monolithic granite slabs. In the south end of the lake reposes an island so aesthetically pleasing that it would be totally appropriate in the garden of a Japanese temple.

Twin Island Lakes to Blue Lake Pass

During the next three or four miles, the High Route traveler traverses one of the most untrammeled sections of the entire 195-mile trek. There are no ducks, no fireplace scars, no bits of trash, and few footprints. It must remain this way.

The routefinding during the next few hours is rather tricky; consult your map often! Many hikers have become temporarily lost in this section.

From the south end of the southern Twin Island Lake, follow a gentle valley 200 yards south to a grass-covered pass offering an extensive view into the glacier-carved valley of the North Fork. Climb the incline west of this pass for several hundred feet, then traverse around the long ridge radiating south from Peak 11,596 (3,528 meters on the Mt. Ritter quad). Ascend diagonally into the valley west of this ridge until reaching a wild and beautiful lake at 10,200 feet (3,100 meters). Continue west across a pleasant basin distinguished by its easy walking.

From a grassy gap north of Peak 10,280 (3,125 meters), ascend a gentle hillside west until level with the top of the peaklet, then contour straight across medium-sized talus until reaching a dark bluff. A fabulous view unfolds at this spot. Below, winding west in graceful curves, lies Bench Canyon, surely one of the most sublime valleys in the range. Minuscule groves of conifers harmonize perfectly with shining slabs and glistening brooks. The view back to the east is equally stunning, for the northern half of the Ritter Range fills the sky. On the escarpment beneath Glacier Lake Pass, the hiker will spy a thin ribbon of white—the endless cascade beside which the hiker recently zigzagged. To the right of lofty Mount Ritter lies spectacular Peak 12,344 (3,734 meters on the Mt. Ritter quad); its jagged crest was not reached until 1964, making it the last major Sierra summit to be climbed. The name Neglected Peak has been suggested.

A moderate descent from the dark bluff leads down into Bench Canyon, and the route for the next mile is both obvious and easy. At the 10,100-foot level—near a stream junction shown on the map—a fairyland setting is encountered. Isolated clumps of whitebark and lodgepole pines rise alongside massive granite boulders, and on the hillside to the north is a twenty-acre meadow that in midseason is blanketed by more wildflowers than the mind can comprehend. Lupine predominates, but there are dozens of other species, including paintbrush, elephant head, pennyroyal, and penstemon. Amid such splendor, it is nearly impossible to avoid cavorting like a child.

At some point the traveler must move on again, forsaking this fertile wonderland for the subalpine zone above. Ascend slabs alongside the south branch of the main creek until coming upon a lake with a prosaic but accurate name: Blue Lake. From here the hiker is afforded an excellent view of the next obstacle on the High Route, the 700-foot climb up to Blue Lake Pass. This saddle—on the eastern boundary of Yosemite National Park—lies to the left of Foerster Peak, which can be identified by its serrated left-hand skyline. Another way to recognize the correct pass is to find the first saddle to the right of a small, brown, U-shaped notch. The ascent to the pass proves amazingly easy, involving grassy slopes, low-angled slabs, and short stretches of stable talus.

From the 11,250-foot pass—the highest High Route elevation reached since Mammoth Crest—the hiker can pause and absorb the extensive view. The entire Ritter Range, jagged and forbidding, lies visible. Michael Minaret, the final resting place of Walter Starr Jr., is remarkably spirelike from this angle. Farther to the south rises an array of the central Sierra's highest summits, including Mounts Abbot, Humphreys, and Goddard. Still farther south, barely visible through the haze, is the isolated Kaweah Peaks Ridge, ninety miles distant.

On the west side of the pass there is an unparalleled panorama of the Clark Range, only seven miles away. Its four major summits are, from left to right, Merced Peak, Red Peak, Gray Peak, and Mount

Clark itself. This latter peak, once known as the Obelisk, was first climbed by that fascinating pioneer, Clarence King. Although King's exploits on Mount Whitney remain far better known than those on Mount Clark, the latter peak was more difficult technically, and King returned to his camp "well pleased that the Obelisk had not vanquished us."

Northwest of the Clark Range, and right of the summit of nearby Peak 11,210, lies Mount Hoffmann, the first major Sierra summit to be climbed and still one of the most popular today. Hidden from the viewer, the Tioga Pass Highway traverses the timbered landscape just south of this peak.

Foerster Peak, the 12,058-foot summit immediately north of Blue Lake Pass, was named in honor of Lewis Foerster, a young cavalryman. In 1895 he was a member of a detachment sent by the federal government to evict the cattlemen and sheepherders who were illegally bringing stock into the fragile landscape of the newly created Yosemite National Park. Thirty-nine years after he had helped patrol this region, Foerster returned with a Sierra Club group and climbed the peak his commanding officer, Lieutenant Nathaniel McClure, had named for him.

Blue Lake Pass to Vogelsang Pass

After taking in the view, drop down steep talus on the west side of Blue Lake Pass; short cliffs intervene occasionally, but they are bypassed easily, especially on the right. After a descent of approximately 400 feet, the hiker arrives on the shores of a rockbound lake. From its outlet, begin a marvelous downhill traverse across subalpine meadowlands occasionally interrupted by streams so clear that the stones on their bottoms glimmer like jewels. (Remember during this descent that no campfires are allowed in Yosemite above the 9,600-foot level.)

Stroll northwest through this idyllic landscape toward the prominent, grass-covered benches lying underneath Peak 11,210. Upon reaching these, turn left and drop down forested bluffs. The Isberg Pass Trail, met in the wide saddle east of Peak 9,958 (9,969 on the Mt. Lyell quad), might be overlooked if the traveler is not watchful, for it is rather inconspicuous in this area. If the members of the party spread out when approaching the saddle, there will be less chance of striding past the trail unknowingly and ending up in Yosemite Valley.

Follow the path north through the dense forest to the nearby dropoff overlooking the vast canyon of the Lyell Fork of the Merced River. During the 950-foot descent through stands of lodgepoles and hemlocks, the hiker gains an excellent view of the park's highest summit, 13,114-foot Mount Lyell. To its left lies the barren, uninteresting basin at the headwaters of Hutching Creek; it is easy to see why the High Route temporarily eschews the subalpine zone in favor of more benign country to the west.

The trail descends the precipitous southern flank of the Lyell Fork Canyon by means of a prominent break in the cliffs, a feature appreciated by Walter Starr, Allen Chickering, and Theodore Solomons in July 1896. These three pioneers had recently embarked on a journey that would prove to be the first complete pack trip ever made between Yosemite and Kings Canyon. Starr called this particular stretch of their route—then trailless, of course—a "perfect ledge . . . made-to-order."

The Lyell Fork can be crossed on any one of several fallen-log bridges. Continue along the trail as it ascends in a gentle manner along another "made-to-order" ledge. Sierra junipers, easily recognized by their massive trunks, line the trail in this section; this is the first High Route appearance of this species since LeConte Canyon. In *The Mountains of California,* John Muir described this tree in a rather unkind fashion: "Its fine color and odd picturesqueness always catch an artist's eye, but to me the Juniper seems a singularly dull and taciturn tree, never speaking to one's heart."

About four miles from the Lyell Fork crossing, the little-used path arrives at the brink of the granite-walled gorge of Lewis Creek. As soon as the trail begins its abrupt descent into this watershed, the traveler catches a glimpse of one of the world's greatest geological wonders, Half Dome; only the upper reaches of this famous formation are visible.

North of the viewer rises another geological oddity, Matthes Crest. Named after noted geologist François Matthes, the airy summit of this serrated white blade of granite has long been the goal of rock climbers.

After meeting a major trail at Lewis Creek, turn right and ascend through the forest. The next few miles prove exceptionally charming, especially to hikers who have spent the preceding days traversing austere timberline country. Lewis Creek—more of a river than a creek—churns frantically down monolithic slabs of granite. The side streams are vigorous also, especially Florence Creek, which provides

The Florence Creek Cascade

the hiker with the most awesome display of cascading water on the entire High Route.

After passing the turnoff to Bernice Lake, the trail ascends through timberline country for about 900 vertical feet to Vogelsang Pass, a grassy saddle containing—until late season—an attractive tarn. The panorama east toward the subalpine basin above Gallison Lake reveals the upper portions of the Mount Lyell group.

Vogelsang Pass to Tuolumne Meadows

The descent from Vogelsang Pass proves trivial, and the hiker soon reaches the shores of Vogelsang Lake. From its outlet, a pleasant locale for a rest stop, the traveler enjoys an all-encompassing view. To the west, eleven miles distant, rises Half Dome; its profile here is the mirror image of the one that multitudes see from Glacier Point. To the northwest, across Fletcher Creek, enormous slabs of exfoliating granite cover acres of landscape; it is easy to understand why this geological curiosity, common in granitic country, often is compared to the layer-by-layer peeling of an onion.

To the right of the peeling granite slabs lie the incongruous cabins of the commercial establishment known as the Vogelsang High Sierra Camp; the American flag waving above the main building seems oddly nationalistic in this wilderness setting. Above the flag, far in the distance, rises the white bulk of the northern Sierra's most prominent landmark, Mount Conness. Its imposing southwest face, visible from Vogelsang Lake, was the first big wall ever climbed in the High Sierra. Warren Harding, fresh from his victory on Yosemite Valley's El Capitan, led this four-day ascent in 1959.

The High Route drops down to the commercial camp, then ascends gently north to broad Tuolumne Pass, the watershed boundary between the Merced and Tuolumne Rivers. From this 10,000-foot saddle an agreeable walk, marred slightly by the increasingly frequent signs of civilization, leads down the forested slopes alongside Rafferty Creek. New regulations forbid camping within four trail miles of Tuolumne Meadows, so plan accordingly.

From the pass follow Rafferty Creek downstream for five miles. Upon intersecting the Muir Trail, turn left and proceed west for three-quarters of a mile to another signed junction. Leave the John Muir Trail—for good—and follow the trail north toward the Tuolumne Meadows Lodge. After 125 yards, this new trail crosses the Lyell Fork of the Tuolumne River at a strikingly beautiful location. The placid water, hitting a barrier of granite, pours through an amazing channel before coursing into the deep green pools below. It is a magical place indeed.

From the bridge head due north (don't follow the obvious path along the river) on a trail for about a third of a mile to a signed junction. Travelers wishing to bypass civilization and continue on the High Route should turn right here and follow the route toward the Gaylor Lakes, as described in the following chapter.

Those wishing to head to Tuolumne should turn left and walk alongside the Dana Fork for 100 yards to a bridge. A short stroll north leads to the Tuolumne Meadows Lodge, the northern terminus of this section of the High Route.

REVERSING THE ROUTE

Since the entire northern portion of this segment of the High Route follows well-marked trails, there should be no routefinding problems when heading south until the hiker is ready to leave the Isberg Pass Trail and begin the cross-country trek toward the Ritter Range. Not long after attaining the valley rim south of the Lyell Fork of the Merced River, the little-used path descends a small bluff and enters a level, forested section. Leave the trail about 300 yards south of the bluff and head due east through the dense forest. After surmounting a short but steep slope, the hiker reaches the grassy benches underneath Peak 11,210. From these, head southeast across meadowlands toward Blue Lake Pass, the conspicuous gap immediately to the right of Foerster Peak. The route across the pass is obvious.

Farther along, it is important to leave Bench Canyon at the correct place; otherwise, numerous cliff bands will be encountered. Quit the main creek at the stream junction shown on the map at 9,700 feet and work diagonally uphill to the east. When above all the cliff bands—at approximately 10,200 feet—begin the long traverse into the basin to the east. The next section, leading to the Twin Island Lakes, loses a few hundred feet of elevation as it circles the ridge dropping from Peak 11,596.

From the outlet of the southern Twin Island Lake, the traveler can pause to study the intimidating headwall leading up to Glacier Lake Pass, the wide gap left of Banner Peak. After leaving the northern lake and contouring around the head of the valley, ascend a steep slope lying 100 yards left of a spectacular cascade. Next, traverse right on a bench over to the creek, meeting it in a solitary grove of pines. Ascend the left branch of the creek to an area of reddish rock high above, then work up and slightly right over complex terrain to Glacier Lake Pass.

There should be little difficulty accomplishing the next several miles over to Cecile Lake, but from its southern shore the hiker may be delayed briefly while searching for the top of the class 3 slot leading down toward Minaret Lake. The key to finding this narrow passage is to proceed to the very lowest point of the lake's "dam," only twenty or thirty feet above water level. A short scouting trip from here quickly reveals the top of the slot and the path below it.

Locating Nancy Pass when traveling south provides the most significant routefinding exercise of this segment of the route. From the bluffs just south of Minaret Lake the hiker can identify Nancy Pass as the first saddle to the left of the large, black, multisummited peak that rises a mile to the south. Another method of verifying the correct pass is that it lies near the junction of the black rock with the red-colored rock that continues east. Once the correct gap has been located, there should be no problem reaching it if one remembers to keep to the right en route, circling the head of the valley.

ALTERNATE ROUTES

It is possible to bypass certain sections of the first part of this segment by using parts of the Muir Trail in conjunction with the spur trails radiating west from it. A study of the map reveals these routes, the most obvious of which is to ignore the Beck Lakes turnoff and instead head up the Minaret Lake Trail, thus avoiding Nancy Pass.

The Ritter Range can be crossed in several places south of Glacier Lake Pass, but because of the enormous elevation drops from these passes into the canyon of the North Fork of the San Joaquin River, such alternate routes are feasible only for strong and exploration-minded backpackers familiar with steep snowfields.

To avoid the traverse—and river crossing—from the Twin Island Lakes to Bench Canyon, follow the unmaintained trail down the North Fork to its junction with Bench Canyon and then head northwest up the canyon. This variation, though not much longer than the High Route, requires an elevation loss—and subsequent gain—of more than 1,000 feet.

In the late season experienced talus walkers can cross the high ridge connecting Foerster and Electra Peaks, thus bypassing Blue Lake Pass. This route lingers longer in the alpine zone than does the High Route and, as an added attraction, passes through one of the loveliest glades in the High Sierra, Lyell Fork Meadow. Nevertheless, this alternate proves far more demanding than the High Route and should be considered only by adventurous backpackers who wish to avoid trails at any cost. Leave the High Route at the dark bluff met prior to the descent into Bench Canyon and travel on a northbound diagonal up into a huge basin. One can cross the crest east of Mount Ansel Adams, a prominent tower not indicated by name on the old map, via a steep, loose gully dropping toward the Lyell Fork of the Merced River. One can also cross the crest immediately west of the first peak west of Electra Peak. These north-facing gullies are safe only in late season, when they are free of snow. After reaching the river, pass west through Lyell Fork Meadow and rejoin the High Route downstream.

MOUNTAINEERING

Pridham Minaret

As mentioned earlier, Minaret Lake provides an excellent base camp for mountaineers. Because of the exceedingly rugged nature of the area, though, there are few peaks that can be climbed by backpackers untrained in the use of the rope and ice ax. There are exceptions, however. To the south of the lake lies Pridham Minaret, the second peaklet from the east on the ridge south of the lake (it isn't named on any map). A scramble up snowfields, gullies, and talus takes the climber to the saddle separating Pridham and Riegelhuth, the easternmost pinnacle. From here a talus slope leads to the 11,000-foot summit, a fine viewpoint. If snow is present anywhere on this route, wait until late afternoon, when the snow has softened.

Volcanic Ridge

An even more spectacular view awaits the hiker who reaches the top of Volcanic Ridge, the 11,501-foot mass immediately north of Minaret Lake. The summit is a popular goal because of this panorama, even though the climb itself is not especially interesting. The usual route begins from the north shore of the lake and ascends a long, grassy slope about 1,100 feet to a saddle. From here turn left and scramble up talus to the summit ridge. Isolated from the main Minaret chain, the peak offers a bird's-eye view perhaps unmatched on the High

Route. The traveler can return via a different route to make a loop trip: from the summit, drop northeast down talus until it becomes feasible to descend a steep slope that levels off in the valley containing the Minaret Mine. Last worked in 1930, the site contains several weathered buildings and numerous tailings attractive to the rock hound. From the isolated mine, head down the creek for nearly half a mile, then turn hard right and ascend a short hill on the west. From its top, follow easy terrain, keeping north of a prominent knoll, back to Minaret Lake.

Mount Ritter

Mount Ritter has been a popular goal of mountaineers for more than a century. Clarence King, that early explorer of the High Sierra—and later the first director of the United States Geological Survey—attempted the enormous peak in 1866 but failed some 500 feet below the top, calling the remaining section "inaccessible." After a thrilling climb, John Muir reached the lofty summit in October 1872. Since then thousands of mountaineers have stood upon the 13,157-foot summit, admiring a panorama that encompasses most of the northern High Sierra.

There are several routes up Mount Ritter's flanks; two of these are feasible for High Route hikers. Muir's descent route—the Southeast Glacier Route—is reached easily from the High Route. Although some glacier travel is encountered, an ice ax is rarely needed, and the ascent is practical for strong backpackers competent on class 3 terrain. Leave the High Route at the bleak tarn at the head of the stream above Ediza Lake and scramble up snow gullies and easy slabs to the glacier, which is mostly hidden from below. Ascend the glacier until it is possible to transfer onto the rocks bordering its northern edge. From here talus slopes—sometimes buried by snow—can be followed easily for the remaining 1,000 feet to the summit.

The second route on Mount Ritter is interesting historically, for it was that peripatetic explorer Theodore Solomons who made the first ascent. Climbing alone in 1892, the twenty-two-year-old carried an 8x10 view camera on the ascent, returning to civilization with the first high-quality photographs ever made in the alpine regions of the High Sierra. His West Slope Route, easier but less interesting than the Southeast Glacier Route, branches from the High Route near Lake Catherine. From the top of the great dropoff overlooking the canyon of the North Fork of the San Joaquin River, work south along a chain of rockbound lakes (called the Ritter Lakes on the new map). From the southernmost lake—called by Solomons "a beautiful sheet of clear water"—ascend talus fans and steep, loose chutes for 2,000 feet to the summit.

Banner Peak

Banner Peak, Mount Ritter's satellite, is also a popular ascent, offering a panorama nearly equal to that of its loftier neighbor. Nearly all climbers ascend the final 1,000-foot slope from the saddle separating the two peaks, but unless the traveler has an ice ax—and knows how to use it—the steep eastern approach to this saddle is not recommended. The far easier northwestern approach leaves the High Route at Lake Catherine and ascends a moderately angled glacier—free of crevasses—all the way to the saddle. Steep talus then leads to the 12,945-foot summit.

Mount Davis

Hikers wary of snowfields and class 2-3 rock will discover that Mount Davis provides an interesting, if less challenging, alternative to Ritter and Banner. Leave the High Route at the northwest edge of Lake

Sunset on peaks, Yosemite National Park

Catherine and ascend a long, easy slope north to the summit plateau.
There is an excellent view of the Mount Lyell group from the 12,311-
foot summit.

Peak 9,988

Surely the easiest climb in proximity to the High Route is Peak 9,988,
a rounded bump slightly south of the southern Twin Island Lake
(3,040+ meters on the Mt. Ritter quad). Although the fifteen-minute
scramble from the shores of the lake hardly qualifies as a bona
fide mountaineering exploit, the view of the Ritter Range and the stupendous canyon of the North Fork make this minor detour from the
High Route a memorable one. The traveler who stands atop this peak
at sundown will marvel at the alpenglow, which for several minutes
illuminates every peak of the Ritter Range.

Foerster Peak

Located north of Blue Lake Pass, Foerster Peak is a class 2-3 scramble
from the saddle. Norman Clyde made the first ascent in 1914 during
one of his earliest forays into the range.

Vogelsang Peak

Another easy climb in proximity to the High Route is Vogelsang Peak.
The traveler can begin either from Vogelsang Pass or Vogelsang Lake;
both routes are class 2. From the 11,516-foot summit one obtains a
marvelous view of the sharp peaks surrounding Tuolumne Meadows.

Chapter Six

CANYON COUNTRY
TUOLUMNE MEADOWS TO TWIN LAKES

There is nothing more fascinating than going "over the top" at a pass—the thrill, the excitement, the mystery of what is beyond! You plod up and up, ever watching your step; over rough rocks, rolling and sliding; over loose, steep shale and sand. You are out of breath; you are weary; the blazing sun beats down upon you; you may say "What's the use?"—when all at once you reach the top and get that grand expansive view and look over into a promised land, on to weird snow-fields, to silvery, flashing streams, down into azure lakes, up to ragged peaks, into the purest air and the bluest of blue skies. It is the call of the high country; the call of the Main Crest; the call toward heaven!

—James Hutchinson,
from the 1923 annual issue of the *Sierra Club Bulletin*

North of the Tioga Road the High Route closely parallels the Sierra crest, never straying more than three miles from it and crossing it on three occasions. Except for the initial few miles and the final two miles, maintained trails are absent from this segment. Thus, for the majority of the trek, the traveler wanders cross-country through varied terrain, surmounting five major ridges along the way. In spite of such up-and-down travel, this segment is not particularly difficult; only one short section—west of Stanton Pass—approaches class 3.

Naturally, talus and snowfields are encountered occasionally, but since these obstacles are not unduly steep, they can be passed quickly by backpackers accustomed to such terrain. Persons not fully acclimated to the heights also will appreciate this segment of the High Route, for only three times does the route penetrate the rarefied atmosphere above the 11,000-foot level.

The scenery along the route is outstanding from the very beginning: the vista south from the Gaylor Lakes includes virtually all the significant peaks in the southern half of Yosemite National Park. Later, from Sky Pilot Col, there is a sterling view of some of northern Yosemite's most conspicuous summits. From this same pass, the panorama in the opposite direction proves equally impressive, for the viewer gazes down upon the colorful metamorphic rock that makes up the eastern flank of this part of the High Sierra.

Near the end of the journey, the traveler becomes intimately involved with two of the most dramatic canyons in the northern Sierra.

White heather (Cassiope mertensiana)

Virginia Canyon, the first of these features, is a remarkably straight glacial trench that drops one vertical mile during its fifteen-mile descent to the Tuolumne River. The High Route crosses Virginia

Canyon near its head, a locale graced by thick forests and meandering brooks.

A few miles farther along, the High Route crosses into Spiller Creek Canyon, another marvelous geographical feature. Although far shorter than Virginia Canyon, this narrow valley is even more beautiful, surrounded as it is by the enormous masses of Whorl Mountain and Virginia Peak. On August 24, 1894, this remote valley was explored by federal cavalry who were attempting to evict sheepherders from the newly established national park. Seeking a passable stock route into nearby Matterhorn Canyon, Lieutenant Nathaniel McClure and several troopers followed Spiller Creek all the way to its source at Horse Creek Pass. For a brief time the High Route exactly follows the track of these pioneers.

Horse Creek Pass occupies an interesting—albeit minor—place in American literature, for it was from here that an exhausted Jack Kerouac watched poet Gary Snyder scramble up the final slopes of Matterhorn Peak, the rocky hulk west of the pass. As recounted in *The Dharma Bums* (in which Snyder is known as Japhy Ryder), Kerouac greeted his victorious friend with these words: "Dammit that yodel of triumph of yours was the most beautiful thing I ever heard in my life. I wish I'd had a tape recorder to take it down." Ryder/Snyder disagrees: "Those things aren't made to be heard by the people below." "By God you're right," Kerouac exclaims, "all those sedentary bums sitting around on pillows hearing the cry of the triumphant mountain smasher, they don't deserve it."

From Horse Creek Pass the final section of the High Route drops 3,500 vertical feet down Horse Creek to Twin Lakes, the northern terminus of the route. During this precipitous descent down yet another stupendous Sierra canyon, the hiker plunges in a matter of hours from the subalpine zone—with its sweeping aprons of granite and patches of minuscule wildflowers—into a less pleasant environment consisting of cars, cabins, sagebrush, and rattlesnakes. This abrupt transformation, typical of all descents down the steep eastern flank of the Sierra, proves especially dramatic to hikers who have remained in timberline country for any length of time. The solitude of such lovely places as Virginia Canyon and Soldier Lake will be recalled wistfully by High Route wanderers who, tramping forlornly through the sordid campground known as Mono Village, know that their journey has ended too suddenly—and too soon.

APPROACHES

This final segment of the High Route begins at Tuolumne Meadows, those verdant acres traversed by the Tioga Road. As mentioned earlier, a ranger station, store, gas station, and campground are found at this popular locale.

Hikers wishing to intersect the High Route partway along this segment can do so by driving to Saddlebag Lake, a reservoir located several miles north of Tioga Pass. One can either join the High Route south of the Conness ridge crossing, or, after following a trail around the reservoir (or taking the boat shuttle across), join the High Route at Cascade Lake.

The northern terminus of the High Route lies at Mono Village, an overly crowded campground located at the west end of Upper Twin Lake. This roadhead is reached easily from U.S. Highway 395 by following a paved road fourteen miles from the town of Bridgeport.

An excellent loop trip is available to hikers who leave cars at Tuolumne Meadows. Follow the High Route until half a mile short of Horse Creek Pass. Leave Spiller Creek at this point and climb up to the prominent saddle south of Matterhorn Peak. From this 11,400-foot pass the traveler is able to descend, in short order, to the trail in upper Matterhorn Canyon. Follow this trail on its circuitous journey south to Glen Aulin, a spectacular meadow on the Tuolumne River. From here a scenic trail leads upriver to Tuolumne Meadows.

The hiker also can depart the High Route at two other locations to join the above-mentioned trail leading to Glen Aulin. Upon reaching Virginia Canyon, simply descend the valley via a path that shortly intersects the main one. The traveler also may descend Spiller Creek Canyon a few miles until meeting the main trail.

THE HIGH ROUTE

Tuolumne Meadows to the Gaylor Lakes

Owing to the configuration of the Tioga Road, various parking lots, and the Dana Fork of the Tuolumne River, this segment of the High Route departs civilization in a rather circuitous fashion. (The following two-mile trail route to the Tioga Road, it should be noted, is feasible only after July 15 most years because the Dana Fork is earlier swollen with snowmelt. If the Dana Fork appears huge, cross it on a bridge near the Tuolumne Meadows Lodge and hike up the Tioga Road several miles to the Gaylor Lakes Trail.)

Stream crossing

Those who plan to leave a car at Tuolumne should do so at the wilderness parking lot, located adjacent to the Tioga Road half a mile east of the bridge that crosses the Tuolumne River. This, and a smaller parking lot a third of a mile toward Tuolumne Lodge, are presently the only long-term parking sites in the area.

Because of recent regulations, camping in the Tuolumne region can be a problem for High Route trekkers. As mentioned in the previous chapter, one is not permitted to camp within four trail miles of Tuolumne Meadows. The Gaylor Lakes region, not far along the High Route, is similarly off-limits. Compounding the problem even further, camping is forbidden in the Hall Natural Area of Inyo National Forest, the region north of the Gaylor Lakes and west of Saddlebag Lake. Since this area and the national park adjoin, one theoretically faces a huge no-camping section—all the way from Tuolumne to Cascade Lake. However, two legal camping possibilities exist to avoid a horrendously long day: one is near the Great Sierra Mine, the other near Spuller Lake. Although specific campsites are not mentioned in this book, the present camping restrictions force an exception to be made here, and both sites will be described at the appropriate place below.

From the wilderness parking area follow the Muir Trail, here mostly paralleling the narrow paved road (not the Tioga Road) leading toward the Tuolumne Meadows Lodge. In a little over half a mile one will come to a bridge spanning the Dana Fork, on the right. Cross this, turn left, and continue on the path upstream for another 100 yards until reaching a marked trail junction. (Hardy through-route travelers coming from Vogelsang and not wishing to stop in civilization will come to this junction from the south and turn right.) Take the left-hand path, the one leading toward the Gaylor Lakes.

Paralleling the creek, the little-used trail alternately surmounts short hills and traverses long, flat wooded sections. After approximately two miles the path abruptly swings left to arrive on the banks of the Dana Fork. Since the park service has not seen fit to build a bridge here, the hiker must wade the twenty-foot-wide brook. Several good fording places will be discovered a short distance upstream; the water, after about July 15, is only a foot or two deep as it courses down flat granite slabs.

The Tioga Road, immediately north of this stream crossing, is the sole road the High Route crosses during its 195-mile length. It may be appropriate here to remember the men and women who fought so long to save the High Sierra from the short-sighted exploiters who, in their quest for timber and minerals, would have built roads and dams in every region. Nowhere else in the continental United States can a person walk such a long distance and come across so few signs of civilization.

The continuation of the trail on the north side of the thirty-foot-wide band of macadam is not immediately obvious; the hiker can discern a trail sign partially hidden in the woods 100 feet north of the highway. (Those who wish to begin their trek here can locate this subtle trail junction most easily by driving east exactly three miles from the highway bridge that spans the Tuolumne River near the store. But remember: no long-term parking is allowed here.)

Follow the winding path north for about 300 yards until it climbs a short hill and meets a dirt road. Turn right and follow this now-abandoned road about 250 yards through open woodlands and meadows until it makes a major curve to the left. At this point, only forty feet from the creek dropping from the Gaylor Lakes, one will spy a confusing sign indicating the way toward Mono Pass. Ignore this. Leave the road here and head up the west side of the creek on a prominent path. This unmarked trail soon begins to climb gently through a forest of lodgepole pines.

Within a mile, the traveler encounters several pocket-sized meadows inundated with corn lilies, a spectacular plant recognized by the enormous oval leaves surrounding its tall, flowering stem. This conspicuous wildflower, mistakenly called skunk cabbage by many eastern hikers, prefers habitats that remain wet throughout the summer.

The rushing creek is never out of earshot during this early section, except in late season. When the roar fades to a whisper, the hiker will know that timberline lies just ahead. Soon the traveler emerges into the splendid meadowlands of the lower portion of the basin containing the three Gaylor and two Granite Lakes. For the first time on this route segment, the High Route hiker obtains an excellent view to the south. Mount Lyell, displaying its ample glacier, dominates the horizon, but the cockscomb pinnacles of the closer Cathedral Range also loom prominently.

The path winds up extensive meadowlands covered with flowers and thousands of granite boulders. Shallow tarns and clumps of lodgepole pines dot the landscape; this is timberline country at its best. All too quickly the traveler comes upon the lowest of the Gaylor Lakes. The trail fades soon after crossing the outlet stream, and the hiker then embarks on a long, trailless section extending nearly all the way to the route's northern terminus. This absence of a trail proves inconsequential at first, for the traveler ascends the easiest possible cross-country terrain almost to the outlet of the lower Granite Lake. This narrow body of water, bordered by granite cliffs and patches of greenery, occupies the bottom of a wide cirque nestled beneath the Sierra crest. Remember: no camping is allowed anywhere in this beautiful basin.

From the outlet stream of the lake ascend the grassy hillside to the northeast, aiming for the low saddle located left of Gaylor Peak, the conspicuous, red-colored hump to the east. During the pleasant stroll toward this landmark, the hiker becomes aware of a significant geological change. Dark chunks of metamorphic rock begin to appear

Storm clouds near the Gaylor Lakes

in the granite-dotted meadows, and by the time the traveler has reached the uppermost Gaylor Lake, reposing directly underneath the steep northern flank of Gaylor Peak, the transformation is complete: slate and other metamorphic rocks have totally replaced the granite. The transition region between the two types of rock, called the contact zone, is often several hundred feet wide and thus indistinct. But where it crosses the Sierra crest north of the Granite Lakes, the border between light and dark is sharply delineated. The High Route parallels this particular contact zone for the remainder of its journey, traversing through granite most of the time, but straying into the more colorful slate occasionally.

Gaylor Lakes to Mine Shaft Pass

From the western shoreline of the highest Gaylor Lake ascend north up the slate-covered hillside, following a prominent path. Soon, on the ridgecrest above, the hiker can spot the ruins of what the map indicates is the Great Sierra Mine. In its heyday the site was known to its owners as the Mount Dana Summit Mine, though considering its distance from Mount Dana, this wasn't the best name. Established in 1878, when traces of silver were discovered nearby, this lode—one of several hundred in an area extending north to Lundy Canyon—was worked in the winter as well as the summer, a fact that explains the buildings' three-foot-thick walls. The winters must have been singularly fierce, especially the one of 1879-80, when a nearby measuring station received nearly 800 inches of snow, double its normal amount. One certainly can empathize with an unnamed miner who descended into the desert town of Bodie one winter to collect the other miners' pay—and who found himself unable to leave the hospitable saloons for several weeks.

It is not known exactly when activity at the Great Sierra Mine ceased, but nearby ventures folded for various reasons in the 1880s. Few of the region's many mines ever turned a profit, and because of its exceedingly remote location, it seems reasonably certain that this one was not financially successful. Nevertheless, the miners left a legacy for present-day hikers, who often stumble across mine shafts, tailings, remnants of buildings, and rusting machinery.

The uppermost ruins of the Great Sierra Mine lie directly astride the Sierra crest, and from this spectacular location the traveler enjoys a fine vista to the south. Mount Dana, three miles distant, looms darkly against the skyline. Closer at hand is the red horn of Gaylor Peak, dominating the highest Gaylor Lake. Farther south, the viewer can distinguish only the summit rocks of Yosemite National Park's highest point, Mount Lyell; most of the mountain remains hidden by a shoulder of Mammoth Peak. Lyell's satellite peaks, including the black cone of Mount Maclure, rise in full view. Also prominent is Vogelsang Peak, recognized by its sharp, pyramidal summit. To its right, some eighteen miles from the mine, the traveler can discern Mount Clark, the guardian of south-central Yosemite.

As mentioned earlier, legal campsites can be discovered near the mine, though one needs to be a Sherlock Holmes to find them. Three prerequisites need to be met: one must be on the north side of the nebulous Sierra crest (and thus out of the park's no-camping zone); be east of the Hall Natural Area (also a no-camping zone); and stray no more than seventy-five yards north of the crest (where a large patch of private property—to safeguard a water supply—means no camping also). The Hall Natural Area boundary here runs along the north-south Range 24/25 line and is marked as a thick line on most maps. Since this line bisects the mine ruins, it follows that anywhere over the crest, off to the right, and not too far north is okay. Adequate spots exist near white outcrops about fifty yards northeast of the uppermost ruin. One may procure water down at the no-camping tarn 150 yards down the slope to the north.

To the north of the Great Sierra Mine one gazes upon a rather unexciting panorama. About the only thing to look at is the next portion of the High Route. The short-term goal is to reach Mine Shaft Pass, the gap 100 feet higher than the Great Sierra Mine and 750 yards north. This minor but important-to-locate High Route landmark lies left of a prominent red knoll and can be further recognized by its color: a small but distinct red and white melange of rock right at the pass.

Contour northwest from the Great Sierra Mine—keeping well above the above-mentioned off-limits tarn—for most of the distance to the pass, then stroll up a short slope, passing an old, filled-in mine shaft, to the saddle. The view north from Mine Shaft Pass more than compensates for the poor northern vista from the Great Sierra Mine. Mount Conness, last seen from the High Route near Tuolumne Pass, can be recognized by the remarkably uniform cliffs that guard its southeastern flank. The sharp upper portion of North Peak protrudes from behind the east ridge of Mount Conness. Directly in line with this landmark, and two-and-a-half miles distant, the viewer can spot a stream cascading from a basin nestled below Mount Conness's east ridge. The High Route traveler will soon be winding up the slabs alongside this ribbon of white water. Also visible from the pass is the southern half of human-enlarged Saddlebag Lake, a popular vacation spot for fishermen.

For the next five miles or so the High Route wanders through beautiful country on the eastern side of the Sierra crest, and Mine Shaft Pass provides a fine opportunity for the hiker to pause and assimilate the dramatic contrasts between the landscapes on either side of the crest. Perhaps it will be the coloration of the peaks that catches the viewer's eye. On much of the eastern side the rounded mountains are composed of reddish-hued slate. But the crest itself and the region west of it are made up of sparkling white granite. The contact zone between these two types of rock is visible here for several miles. The vegetation provides another contrast, for there is a relative scarcity of large trees on the eastern flank of the Sierra. Since the crest acts as a barrier to the prevailing storm track, most of the winter's precipitation falls on the western slope of the range. When looking at Tioga Crest, immediately east of Saddlebag Lake, the viewer is gazing upon a desert mountain.

Mine Shaft Pass to Cascade Lake

Descend about 125 vertical feet from Mine Shaft Pass to a dropoff overlooking meadows far below, then move left onto a reddish-colored bench below an all-year snowfield. Continue traversing in the direction of Mount Conness; soon one will encounter a white, slabby section with a few class 2-3 problems. This section quickly leads to easier terrain, gray metamorphic rock sprinkled with dwarfed whitebark pines. Now drop down into a meadow and follow a "hidden" valley down to the north. When this steepens radically, leave it and contour left on easy terrain, again heading in the direction of Conness. Soon one spies a portion of Spuller Lake down and to the northwest; easy but roundabout terrain takes one down to the outlet.

Although camping is forbidden in this area (and all the way to Cascade Lake), there is a legal spot fairly close by, though not on the High Route. From Spuller's outlet follow the creek down to Fantail Lake, which is turned on the left. From its outlet walk about 300 yards downstream along a good path. Here one will see a sign indicating the border of the Hall Natural Area. Camping is legal below here, and anywhere to the east. Although this area lies about a mile off the High Route, what's a twenty-five minute detour through beautiful country if a campsite is sorely needed?

Circle lovely Spuller Lake on the east and pass through the saddle west of Peak 10,493 (10,520+ on the Tioga Pass quadrangle). Continue north across the narrow strip of meadow separating Green Treble Lake from its placid eastern neighbor, then stroll down into the idyllic meadows that blanket the floor of a large basin. Considering its proximity to the Saddlebag Lake Road, this fabulous cirque, with its near-perfect proportions of pine, granite, and water, remains curiously untrammeled. A similar site in the Alps undoubtedly would contain a large hut, a network of eroded trails radiating from it, and copious quantities of trash.

The High Route hiker next embarks on the most alpine section of the route since Blue Lake Pass. Although the crossing of the east ridge of Mount Conness is not particularly difficult, it contains all the ingredients for a thrilling adventure: firm granite, airy traverses, and stunning views. From the basin ascend north up grass-covered ramps and gullies alongside the cascading stream that originates near the ridge far above. After a gentle climb of some 800 feet—during which time there are excellent views of Mount Dana and its drab companion, Mount Gibbs—the hiker arrives at an extensive flat area at 10,900 feet. To the northeast, about a quarter of a mile distant, lies a broad, grassy saddle. But instead of aiming for this obvious gap, turn slightly left and proceed due north up a rocky slope that ends on the east ridge of Mount Conness.

Greeting the hiker who accomplishes this short climb to an appalling dropoff is a bird's-eye panorama. Below repose dozens of lakes, some of which lie directly on the contact zone between the granite and the slate. On Saddlebag Lake, anglers' boats scuttle about like water beetles on a pond. North Peak's amazingly sharp summit horn towers prominently to the northwest; below it lie several of the rockbound Conness Lakes. To the right of North Peak rises the serrated mass known as Shepherd Crest; the High Route soon crosses Sky Pilot Col, the saddle to its right. Farther right, the stark ocher- and rust-colored cliffs at the head of Lundy Canyon provide another dramatic reminder that the traveler stands on the Sierra's eastern flank.

After assimilating this magnificent view, do not become discouraged when trying to pick out the next section of the High Route. The hiker's instincts rebel at the thought of descending the steep cliff below, and this proves to be the correct decision. Instead, turn west and scramble up the aesthetic east ridge of Mount Conness for several hundred feet until, at about 11,300 feet, it meets a conspicuous curving spur that drops abruptly toward the lowest Conness Lake (shown as Lake 10,613 on the Tioga Pass quad). This providentially situated class 2 spur affords a spectacular and direct route to the lake below.

Leave the ridgecrest of Mount Conness and carefully cross low-angled slabs and snowpatches until reaching the top of the curving spur. Zigzag down this feature for approximately 700 feet to the pleasant meadows near the outlet of the lowest Conness Lake. At this point the hiker stands close to the tumultuous cascade that plunges into the basin containing Greenstone Lake.

The next High Route obstacle proves tame in comparison to the crossing of Mount Conness's east ridge. Although North Peak's east ridge must be crossed, it is surprisingly gentle, rising only 100 feet

Tarn near Mount Conness, early season

above the creek. Surmount this rounded hump at any of several possible places and descend its steeper northern flank to the flat, rocky
terrain leading north to Cascade Lake. Camping becomes legal again
250 yards south of the lake, but no campfires are allowed in the area.

This pleasant site, with its striking juxtaposition of water, granite, and meadow, proves to be an excellent spot to pause and admire
the effects of glaciation. The traveler need not be an expert in glaciol-
ogy to discern traces of the ice sheet's passage, for they are everywhere. For instance, hundreds of glacial erratics cover the acres of
slabs. These enormous chunks of rock, transported from afar by the
moving ice, were marooned when the ice finally melted, some 10,000
years ago. Irregularly shaped patches of glacier-polished rock are visible from long distances, and these can reflect so much light that
even in a region where all is brightness the traveler must quickly
avert his or her eyes. By examining these glass-smooth slabs more
intimately, the hiker can discover two further signs of the glacier's

passage. Parallel striations show the exact direction in which the ice flowed, dragging with it pebbles of harder rock. Semicircular nicks in the granite show where large stones, under colossal pressure from the weight of the ice, preyed upon weaknesses in the bedrock and chipped fragments loose. These "chatter marks" also indicate the direction in which the ice flowed.

Cascade Lake to Shepherd Lake

From the north end of Cascade Lake follow a decent path that meanders up the pleasant timberline country rising to the north. At approximately 10,900 feet the traveler arrives at a shallow tarn known as Secret Lake. Above its rocky shores it is possible to pick out the next High Route pass, Sky Pilot Col. This gap, located immediately to the right of the talus-covered mass of Shepherd Crest, lies only 700 feet above Secret Lake. But the terrain leading upward to the pass proves far more rugged than the previous section, with talus and scree replacing grassy hillsides.

The route to Sky Pilot Col can be divided into three distinct sections. The initial obstacle, a fairly stable talus slope, involves an elevation gain of about 300 feet and leads to the bottom of a shallow bowl devoid of vegetation. Next, a stretch of ever-steepening talus leads up the left side of this bowl to the final indignity, a short but steep scree slope that most hikers will find offensive.

Sky Pilot Col, at 11,650 feet, is the highest point reached by the High Route since Gabbot Pass. I named this gap on the Sierra crest for the conspicuous blue flower that blankets the entire saddle in midseason. The fragrant sky pilot, or polemonium, grows only above 11,000 feet, and Sierra mountaineers long have regarded it as the symbol of the alpine zone.

As one might expect, the views from this high perch are extensive. Numerous lakes dot the foreground landscape; the largest of these is Saddlebag Lake, here seen in its entirety. Especially dramatic is the north side of North Peak, where high-angle snow couloirs slice a spectacular cliff. Far to the south, twenty-two miles distant, rises the dark horn of Banner Peak, last seen from Blue Lake Pass. Looking in the opposite direction, the viewer gazes across the glaciated trench of Virginia Canyon toward several noteworthy peaks. Most conspicuous, by reason of its coloration, is Virginia Peak; the traveler easily can see why its official name was once Red Peak (the name was changed in the mid-1950s to avoid confusion with the Red Peak of the Clark Range). Behind this rust-colored pyramid rises northern Yosemite's highest point, Matterhorn Peak. To its left lies Whorl Mountain, recognized by its steep, rugged east face. Directly in line with this prominent feature is Soldier Lake, perched on a shelf and completely surrounded by granite. The High Route soon reaches this rarely visited body of water. In the foreground, only a mile away, the viewer can discern a portion of Shepherd Lake, the next High Route objective.

The 1,300-foot descent from Sky Pilot Col to Shepherd Lake is not technically difficult, yet the traveler cannot relax for a single step: the terrain demands constant attention. The talus, although not particularly steep, tends to be unstable, for the hiker scrambles down slate, not granite. Year-round snowfields, when soft, offer short stretches of glissading, but the sight of the sharp rocks lurking below serves as a constant reminder not to lose control.

During the course of this less-than-pleasant descent, the traveler will almost certainly spot flocks of tiny birds flitting about the snowfields. The gray-crowned rosy finch, one of the only birds to be found in the Sierra above 11,000 feet, roams the surface of the snow in search of insects. After observing these active inhabitants of the subalpine zone, John Muir commented that they "always have a white tablecloth for their meals."

Shepherd Lake to Stanton Pass

At Shepherd Lake the terrain changes abruptly; from a world consisting solely of rock and snow, the traveler steps instantly into a region of meadows and willows. In fact, willows so choke the stream below the lake that the hiker might be temporarily stymied by their wiry branches. The solution, luckily, is not hard to figure out: simply walk down the left, or west, side of the brook, keeping at least 100 feet away from the watercourse. In this manner it is possible to avoid the most sinister tangles of willow, instead traversing through normal timberline country.

When about one-half mile below Shepherd Lake, one enters a forest of hemlocks and lodgepole pines. Shortly below here, the willows begin to choke the entire valley, and the traveler realizes that it is time to flee; the High Route, after all, is not a jungle trek. At about the 10,000-foot level, cross the stream and angle to the right in the this descent study the next High Route obstacle, Sky Pilot Col; it lies near the head of the major canyon seen directly across the glacial trench. The pass also is visible from the outlet of Shepherd Lake; the correct notch lies to the right of a huge, squarish block that leans to the right.

The traveler encounters no further routefinding problems until reaching the environs of Mount Conness. From the outlet of the lowest of the Conness Lakes ascend south up a prominent rounded spur leading to the east ridge of Mount Conness. When nearing this imposing ridgecrest, avoid the temptation to traverse left too soon, for steep snowfields lurk here until late season. Instead, continue upward until it becomes safe to move left onto the ridgecrest.

Drop east down this crest for a few hundred feet, then leave it and head south down gentle country until reaching the tree-covered basin far below. Continue south across superb timberline country to the broad saddle overlooking Spuller Lake. Here the traveler obtains an excellent vista of the next section of the High Route. More or less directly in line with Mount Dana, and about one-and-a-half miles away, lies an inconspicuous, reddish-colored knoll. The next High Route col—Mine Shaft Pass—can be seen just right of the knoll. During most of the traverse to the pass, the red knoll is superimposed upon Mount Dana, thus simplifying the routefinding.

From Mine Shaft Pass curve south half a mile to the crest of the Sierra, a wide pass marked by the ruins of the Great Sierra Mine. From this historic site the hiker should have little trouble finding the correct route down to the Tioga Road.

ALTERNATE ROUTES

The topography of this part of the Sierra dictates that the High Route follow a fairly rigid course. In fact, only one alternate route is obvious: the bypass of Sky Pilot Col. Although this variation is less direct and involves stretches of bushwhacking, it also avoids a significant section of talus—a fact that some hikers may appreciate.

Leave the High Route shortly after passing Cascade Lake and follow a crude path up and left along a series of class 2 ledges until reaching the extreme northern end of the half-mile-long saddle stretching between North Peak and Shepherd Crest. From this 11,200-foot saddle, known as McCabe Pass, or Secret Lake Pass, a well-defined path winds down 700 vertical feet to the beautiful meadowlands a quarter of a mile northeast of Upper McCabe Lake.

Leave the path at the meadows and strike west, soon dropping down a willow-choked valley toward McCabe Creek, located in the prominent wooded canyon far below. Leave the creek at the 9,700-foot level and climb a gentle slope up and right to the low, wide saddle northeast of Peak 10,085. From this pass work diagonally down through a dense forest until reaching the floor of Virginia Canyon. The High Route is joined a mile or so upstream, when almost under the cliffs of Gray Butte.

MOUNTAINEERING

Lembert Dome

Lembert Dome is not only one of the most attractive features of the Tuolumne Meadows region, it also offers the hiker an easy climb capped by a superb view. On a summer's day the climber is likely to share its rounded summit with numerous other adventurers, for the prominent formation lures hikers from the nearby campground. The dome was named after John Baptist Lembert, a hermit who in the late 1880s homesteaded a small parcel of land surrounding the soda springs west of the dome. At this idyllic site Lembert raised angora goats until a severe winter depleted his stock; afterward, he collected butterflies and botanical specimens for museums. In 1896 Lembert was murdered by a robber at his winter quarters below Yosemite Valley.

The top of the dome can be reached quickly from the vicinity of the Tuolumne Meadows Lodge. Follow the marked trail toward Dog Lake until reaching a ridge several hundred feet above the Tioga Road. Leave the path here and stroll west through open woodlands to the massive granite slabs that make up the summit area.

Gaylor Peak

Another easy-to-reach landmark offering a fine view is Gaylor Peak. This 11,004-foot mass, composed of reddish slate, is climbed most easily via its gently angled south ridge. Lying less than one mile from Tioga Pass, it too is likely to have a teeming summit on a midafternoon in August.

Mount Conness

As the highest crest peak north of the Tioga Road, Mount Conness naturally offers the climber a sterling viewpoint. All of Yosemite's

TOPOGRAPHIC MAPS

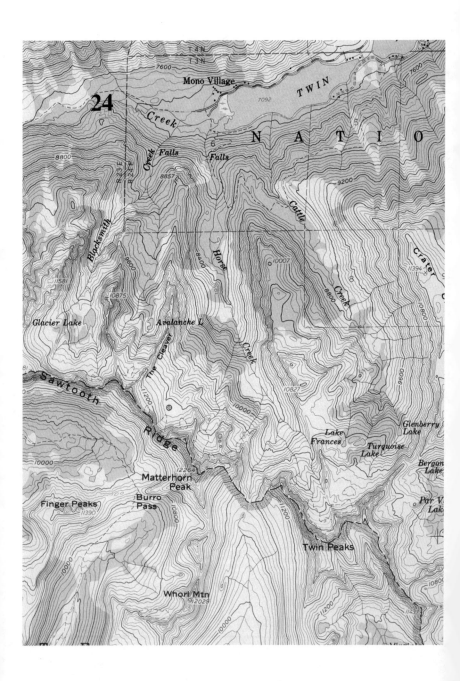

Bibliography

Listed below are those books and articles that contain material quoted in the text. Page numbers are omitted; readers will have no trouble finding the quotes if they use a table of contents or an index to home in on the relevant prose.

Badè, William Frederic. "On the Trail with the Sierra Club." *Sierra Club Bulletin* 5, no. 1 (January 1904).

Bedayan, Raffi. "Mountaineering Notes: The Rock-Climbers' Knapsack Trip." *Sierra Club Bulletin* 24, no. 3 (June 1939).

Brown, Bolton Coit. "A Trip About the Headwaters of the South and Middle Forks of Kings River." *Sierra Club Bulletin* 1, no. 8 (May 1896).

———. "Wanderings in the High Sierra Between Mt. King and Mt. Williamson." *Sierra Club Bulletin* 2, no. 1 (January 1897).

Bunn, G. R. "An Ascent of Mount Humphreys." *Sierra Club Bulletin* 11, no. 1 (January 1920).

Colby, William E. "Editorial: Proposed Enlargement of the Sequoia National Park." *Sierra Club Bulletin* 12, no. 3 (1926).

———. "Twenty-nine Years with the Sierra Club." *Sierra Club Bulletin* 16, no. 1 (February 1931).

Cowles, Elizabeth S. "Have You a Mountain Widow in Your Home?" *Sierra Club Bulletin* 34, no. 6 (June 1949).

Farquhar, Francis P. *Place Names of the Sierra Nevada.* San Francisco: Sierra Club, 1926.

———. "The Story of Mount Whitney." *Sierra Club Bulletin* 14, no. 1 (February 1929).

———. *Up and Down California in 1860-64: The Journal of William H. Brewer.* New Haven: Yale University Press, 1930.

Fincher, Mark. Letter to author, August 8, 1996.

Frémont, John C. *Memoirs of My Life.* Chicago: Belford, Clarke & Co., 1886.

Gompertz, Helen. "Up and Down Bubb's Creek." *Sierra Club Bulletin* 2, no. 2 (May 1897).

Hutchinson, J. S., Jr. "First Ascent: Mount Humphreys." *Sierra Club Bulletin* 5, no. 3 (January 1905).

———. "A New Link in the John Muir Trail: Palisade Creek–Mather Pass." *Sierra Club Bulletin* 11, no. 4 (1923).

Hutchinson, Lincoln. "Red-and-White Peak and the Headwaters of Fish Creek." *Sierra Club Bulletin* 4, no. 3 (February 1903).

Kerouac, Jack. *The Dharma Bums.* New York: Viking Press, 1958.

King, Clarence. *Mountaineering in the Sierra Nevada.* Boston: J. R. Osgood and Company, 1872.

LeConte, Joseph N. "The Basin of the South Fork of the San Joaquin River." *Sierra Club Bulletin* 2, no. 5 (January 1899).

———. "Among the Sources of the South Fork of King's River." *Sierra Club Bulletin* 4, no. 3 (February 1903).

———. "The Ascent of the North Palisades." *Sierra Club Bulletin* 5, no. 1 (January 1904).

———. "Diary, 1904." Bancroft Library LeConte Collection, University of California, Berkeley, Calif.

———. "The Evolution Group of Peaks." *Sierra Club Bulletin* 5, no. 3 (January 1905).

———. "The High Mountain Route Between Yosemite and the King's River Cañon." *Sierra Club Bulletin* 7, no. 1 (January 1909).

Lipman, Robert L. "The 1935 Outing." *Sierra Club Bulletin* 21, no. 1 (February 1936).

Matthes, François E. "The Devils Postpile and its Strange Setting." *Sierra Club Bulletin* 15, no. 1 (February 1930).

Michael, C. W. "First Ascent of the Minarets." *Sierra Club Bulletin* 12, no. 1 (1924).

Monroe, Harriet. "Camping Above the Yosemite—A Summer Outing with the Sierra Club." *Sierra Club Bulletin* 7, no. 2 (June 1909).

Muir, John. *The Mountains of California.* New York: The Century Co., 1894.

Parsons, Marion Randall. "The Grand Cañons of the Tuolumne and the Merced." *Sierra Club Bulletin* 6, no. 4 (January 1908).

Robinson, Doug. "Running Talus." Sidebar in the *Great Pacific Iron Works Catalog.* Ventura, Calif.: Chouinard Equipment, 1976.

Rockwell, Bob. Unpublished giardia report in possession of author, dated March 2, 1996.

Schumacher, Genny, ed. *Deepest Valley: A Guide to Owens Valley.* San Francisco: Sierra Club, 1962.

Solomons, Theodore S. "Among the Sources of the San Joaquin." *Sierra Club Bulletin* 1, no. 3 (January 1894).

———. "A Search for a High Mountain Route from the Yosemite to the King's River Cañon." *Sierra Club Bulletin* 1, no. 6 (May 1895).

———. "Mt. Goddard and its Vicinity—in the High Sierra of California." *Appalachia* 8 (January 1896).

———. "Unexplored Regions of the High Sierra: The Sources of the San Joaquin." *Overland Monthly* 27 (May 1896).

———. "Unexplored Regions of the High Sierra: The Sources of the King's River." *Overland Monthly* 27 (June 1896).

———. "An Early Summer Excursion to the Tuolumne Cañon and Mt. Lyell." *Sierra Club Bulletin* 2, no. 1 (January 1897).

———. "The Beginnings of the John Muir Trail." *Sierra Club Bulletin* 25, no. 1 (February 1940).

Starr, Walter A. "From Yosemite to Kings River Canyon." *Sierra Club Bulletin* 20, no. 1 (February 1935).

Starr, Walter A., Jr. *Guide to the John Muir Trail and the High Sierra Region.* 12th revised edition. San Francisco: Sierra Club, 1974.

Twain, Mark. *Roughing It.* Hartford, Conn.: American Publishing Co., 1872.

Versteeg, Chester. "The Peaks and Passes of the Upper Basin, South Fork of the Kings River." *Sierra Club Bulletin* 11, no. 4 (1923).

INDEX

About the Author

Steve Roper has been a climbing buff for over 45 years, beginning his career as a young boy in 1950 at Lassen Peak. He has climbed 180 separate routes in Yosemite Valley, including three on El Capitan, and made ascents of ninety named Sierra peaks. Steve's achievements also include marching behind two Nobel laureates across the Pettus Bridge in Selma, Alabama; serving in the Army for two years and in Vietnam for seven months; and becoming an award-winning author.

Steve is the author of ten books, including the 1994 Banff Festival of Books' award-winning *Camp 4: Recollections of a Yosemite Rockclimber,* and co-author of *Fifty Classic Climbs in North America.* He received The Sierra Club's Francis Farquhar Award in 1983 and The American Alpine Club's Literary Award in 1995. As associate editor for the past five years of *Summit* magazine, Steve merges his mountain experiences regularly with his writing. He resides in Oakland, California.

THE MOUNTAINEERS, founded in 1906, is a nonprofit outdoor activity and conservation club, whose mission is "to explore, study, preserve, and enjoy the natural beauty of the outdoors. . . . " Based in Seattle, Washington, the club is now one of the largest such organizations in the United States, with seven branches throughout Washington State.

The Mountaineers sponsors both classes and year-round outdoor activities in the Pacific Northwest, which include hiking, mountain climbing, ski-touring, snowshoeing, bicycling, camping, kayaking and canoeing, nature study, sailing, and adventure travel. The club's conservation division supports environmental causes through educational activities, sponsoring legislation, and presenting informational programs. All club activities are led by skilled, experienced volunteers, who are dedicated to promoting safe and responsible enjoyment and preservation of the outdoors.

If you would like to participate in these organized outdoor activities or the club's programs, consider a membership in The Mountaineers. For information and an application, write or call The Mountaineers, Club Headquarters, 7700 Sand Point Way NE, Seattle, WA 98115; (206) 521-6001.

The Mountaineers Books, an active, nonprofit publishing program of the club, produces guidebooks, instructional texts, historical works, natural history guides, and works on environmental conservation. All books produced by The Mountaineers are aimed at fulfilling the club's mission.

Send or call for our catalog of more than 500 outdoor titles:

 The Mountaineers Books
1001 SW Klickitat Way, Suite 201
Seattle, WA 98134
800-553-4453
mbooks@mountaineersbooks.org
www.mountaineersbooks.org